CW01082778

Waiting In Faith

Trusting God in Times of Uncertainty

Sage Wisdom

Artificial Intelligence

Welcome to a book crafted with the assistance of artificial intelligence. As AI continues to revolutionize the way content is created, I am excited to present this unique literary work. Embracing the innovative capabilities of AI, this book represents a new chapter in the evolution of storytelling. I invite you to immerse yourself in this one-of-a-kind reading experience and witness the intersection of technology and creativity.

Dedication

To Christina,

Whose unwavering prayers, encouragement, and support have been my guiding light. Thank you for believing in me and helping me through every challenge. This journey is as much yours as it is mine. Your kindness and strength inspire me every day.

Thank You

- If this book resonates with you, please consider leaving a review. Your feedback helps guide other readers and supports a meaningful cause.

- All profits from the sales of this book are donated to charities that impact lives.

- Subscribe to the mailing list at sagewisdombooks.com for monthly updates on new releases!

Contents

Introduction

L et's face it—waiting is tough. It's as much a part of our lives as breathing, but that doesn't mean we enjoy it. We've all been there: stuck in traffic, counting the minutes until payday, waiting for test results, or agonizingly refreshing email inboxes. The waiting game can be downright exasperating. But before you toss this book aside thinking it's just another sermon on patience, bear with me; I promise we'll dive into these waters together, buoyed by humor and a dash of camaraderie.

Waiting is not only inevitable but also a universal experience that knits us together as human beings. It's perfectly natural to feel an array of emotions—frustration, anxiety, doubt, maybe even anger. You're not alone in this rollercoaster of feelings. Many have grappled with similar sentiments. So here's the good news: together, we're going to uncover the beauty that can emerge in these seasons of waiting. It's high time we flipped the script, transforming what feels like lost time into something profoundly beautiful.

Now, think about waiting on God in particular. This might seem like a passive endeavor at first glance, but let's set the record straight—it's anything but passive. Picture it more as an active engagement of faith and trust. It's like planting a seed. Without time and care, that tiny seed will never grow into a robust plant. Similarly, our spiritual journeys require patience and nurturing—often when we least expect it. It's during these interludes that our faith deepens, our character strengthens, and our resilience shines.

Imagine being part of a community that truly gets it. A group where you can share your waiting stories, find solace in others' experiences, and cultivate a support system that uplifts you during challenging times. Picture it: a room full of people nodding along as you recount your struggles, chime in with understanding laughs, and offer encouraging words. You'll see, you are stronger than you think—and even stronger together.

Take a moment now to pause and reflect. Seriously, put this book down for just a second. What areas of your life are you currently waiting on? Maybe it's a promotion at work, clarity on a major decision, healing from an illness, or finding that right someone. Can this period of waiting become an opportunity for growth, for digging deeper into your own soul and connecting with God in ways you hadn't imagined before? Your journey of waiting can be a powerful catalyst for change, turning downtime into prime time.

But wait, there's more! Throughout this book, you'll discover practical techniques designed to guide you through your waiting experiences. Yes, you read that right—13 tools and strategies crafted to turn your perspective upside-down. From mastering the art of developing patience to actively engaging with God's promises, each chapter offers unique insights that will inspire you to view waiting not as wasted time but as a vital part of your spiritual journey. Intrigued? You should be.

Here's the kicker: we live in a fast-paced, impatient society. Everything around us screams instant gratification. We tap, swipe, click, and scroll our way through life, expecting immediate results for everything—from food delivery to relationships. In such a world, waiting can feel like an unnatural burden, a glitch in the matrix of modern living. Yet, what if we viewed waiting not as a setback, but as an essential path to deeper faith and fulfillment? Together, we'll explore this paradigm shift, debunking the myth that waiting is synonymous with stagnation or failure.

So, let's embark on this journey with open hearts and minds. Let's laugh at our shared frustrations, find strength in each other's stories, and embrace the waiting periods with newfound intention and grace. At the end of the day, waiting doesn't have to be something you merely survive—it can be something you thrive through.

With that said, grab a cozy blanket, a cup of your favorite beverage, and settle in. You're about to learn that waiting, with all its ups and downs, can actually lead to some of the most profound, funny, and transformative moments of your life. Welcome to the adventure of waiting. Ready? Let's dive in.

Chapter One

Understanding the Waiting

Waiting on God can often feel like being in the longest line at the DMV, minus the paper ticket and lukewarm coffee. It's a concept that might seem straightforward but comes packed with more layers than a five-tiered cake. This chapter invites you to uncover what waiting truly means through a biblical lens, promising more than just a passive thumb-twiddling experience. Instead of seeing waiting as downtime, imagine it as a divine intermission where the stage is set for something remarkable. While society views waiting with the same enthusiasm reserved for watching paint dry, you'll discover it's anything but tedious when trust in God's timing enters the mix.

In this chapter, we'll dive headfirst into how the Bible redefines waiting, transforming it from a passive bore into an active engagement filled with faith and hope. We'll explore inspirational stories of ancient figures who mastered the art of waiting—and not just any waiting, but waiting with purpose and patience. You'll also get a glimpse into modern-day applications, where your own periods of waiting could become transformative spiritual experiences. Buckle up because by the end of this chapter, you might just find yourself looking forward to the next time you have to wait!

Defining Waiting from a Biblical Perspective

Waiting is a concept deeply embedded in the Christian faith and richly illustrated throughout the Bible. Often, waiting is seen as a passive state, but in the realm of spirituality, it bears a far deeper significance. Understanding the biblical context of waiting reveals that it intertwines closely with hope and reliance on God's perfect timing.

In scriptures, waiting is not portrayed as an idle or wasted time. Rather, it is often linked to a hopeful expectation of God's intervention. For instance, Psalm 27:14 instructs, "Wait for the Lord; be strong and take heart and wait for the Lord." This shows that biblical waiting is about trusting God's plan and timing, even when the path ahead is unclear. It's a heart posture that leans heavily on divine wisdom rather than human understanding.

When we examine the difference between passive and active waiting, we find that biblical waiting calls for an active approach. Passive waiting might resemble someone sitting in a doctor's office, flipping through magazines until called. Active waiting, however, is like a gardener who plants seeds and faithfully tends to them, anticipating growth even when there's no immediate sign of it. Isaiah 40:31 beautifully captures this notion: "But those who hope in the Lord will renew their strength. They will soar on wings like eagles; they will run and not grow weary, they will walk and not faint." This verse underscores that waiting involves renewed strength, purposeful action, and continuous trust in God's provision.

Consider the endurance of the saints, a theme resonant throughout the Bible. Many prominent figures faced long periods of waiting before God's promises were fulfilled. Take Abraham, for example, who waited many years for the birth of his son Isaac after God promised him numerous descendants. His story exemplifies the virtue of patience and steadfast faith, despite long delays. Similarly, Moses waited 40 years in the desert before leading the Israelites out of Egypt, emphasizing that waiting often precedes significant moments of divine revelation and action.

Furthermore, examining cultural views on waiting highlights a stark contrast between modern perspectives and biblical teachings. Today's society often sees waiting as a nuisance or a barrier to efficiency. We're conditioned to expect instant gratification, whether it's rapid delivery services or quick search results online. Our fast-paced world shudders at the thought of enduring long periods without immediate rewards.

Biblical teachings, however, reframe waiting as an opportunity for spiritual growth and reliance on God. This dichotomy invites believers to view waiting through a spiritual lens, recognizing it as a phase where God works profoundly within us. For instance, contemporary frustrations such as waiting for career advancements, life partners, or personal breakthroughs can be reframed as seasons of preparation. In these times, God cultivates character, faith, and readiness for future blessings (https://facebook.com/faithstrongtoday, 2021).

To gain a deeper understanding, let's delve into some practical examples and experiences. Imagine a person awaiting a job promotion. While it's easy to become disheartened, active waiting involves honing new skills, seeking mentorship, and trusting that God is orchestrating the right opportunity at the right time. This period isn't merely an inconvenient delay but a crucial phase of growth and preparation for greater responsibilities.

Likewise, consider someone praying for healing from a prolonged illness. The natural inclination might be to become weary and frustrated. However, active waiting means engaging in consistent prayer, exploring medical options, and leaning on community support while trusting in God's healing power.

The beauty of biblical waiting lies in its capacity to teach humility and patience. As humans, our desire for control often clashes with the necessity to wait, revealing our limitations. Yet, through waiting, we learn to surrender our anxieties and ambitions to God, developing a deeper sense of humility. As Psalm 37:7 advises, "Be still before the Lord and wait patiently for him." This stillness isn't inactivity but a peaceful heart posture assured of God's sovereign control.

Moreover, waiting fosters patience—a quality much needed but seldom cultivated in our hurried lives. Patience keeps us grounded, reduces stress, and aligns our expectations with God's timeline. It shifts our focus from what we want now to the greater purpose and timing God has planned for us.

Common Emotional Struggles Associated with Waiting

Waiting on God is an integral part of the Christian journey, but it brings with it a host of emotional challenges that can be difficult to navigate. The act of waiting naturally stirs up a myriad of feelings, from frustration and impatience to fear and isolation. Understanding these emotions helps believers process their experiences, allowing them to grow spiritually even during periods of uncertainty.

One of the most common emotional responses to waiting is frustration. When things don't happen according to our timeline, it's easy to become restless and impatient. This frustration can manifest in various ways, such as irritability, resentment, or even anger. We live in a world where instant gratification is the norm, making the patience required by waiting on God's timing feel especially exasperating. It's crucial to acknowledge this sense of frustration rather than suppressing it. By doing so, one can seek solace in prayer, asking God for strength and patience to endure the waiting period.

Accompanying frustration often is the fear of the unknown. When waiting for something significant, such as a job opportunity, a relationship, or a health outcome, the future's uncertainty can be overwhelming. This fear might lead to anxiety about what lies ahead and whether the awaited outcome will ever come to fruition. These fears are not only natural but also provide an opportunity to deepen one's trust in God's plan. Instead of being paralyzed by fear, believers can turn to scripture and remind themselves of God's promises to never leave nor forsake them (Hebrews 13:5).

Another profound emotional challenge during waiting is the feeling of isolation. Extended periods of waiting can make individuals feel as though they are alone in their struggles, cut off from others who are moving forward with their lives. This perceived isolation can intensify feelings of loneliness and despair. However, it's important to remember that everyone has their seasons of waiting. Sharing one's experience with trusted friends, family, or faith communities can provide much-needed support and encouragement. Moreover, engaging in prayer and meditation allows individuals to connect more deeply with God, finding comfort in His presence even when human companionship feels distant.

Lastly, waiting often stirs a growing spiritual hunger. As people wait, they may find themselves yearning more intensely for closeness with God. This longing for spiritual intimacy can act as a catalyst for growth, driving believers to seek deeper connections through practices like regular prayer, scripture reading, and worship. This hunger isn't just about filling time; it's about transforming the waiting period into a spiritually enriching experience. By drawing nearer to God, individuals can find purpose and meaning in their waiting, seeing it not as wasted time but as a season ripe for personal and spiritual development.

Initial Steps to Embrace Waiting as a Spiritual Practice

When faced with the challenge of waiting on God, many Christians find themselves struggling to integrate this process into their spiritual disciplines. It's not merely about twiddling one's thumbs but rather engaging in a purposeful and faith-filled journey. To help you navigate this path, here are some practical initial steps that can make the waiting experience an enriching part of your spiritual life.

Practicing Mindfulness in Waiting

Mindfulness is about being fully present in the moment, aware of where we are and what we're doing. For those in a period of waiting, practicing mindfulness means fostering an awareness of God's presence throughout the wait. Instead of focusing on the end goal or the object of your wait, turn your attention to what God might be teaching you right now. Use deep breathing exercises to center yourself whenever you feel anxious or impatient. This practice doesn't just keep you calm; it opens up space for listening to God's voice in your life.

Establishing a Waiting Journal

One powerful tool for integrating waiting into your spiritual discipline is establishing a waiting journal. (Kathy, 2016) Keeping a record of thoughts, prayers, and observations during waiting periods serves multiple purposes. It helps maintain concentration and focus during Bible reading, meditation, and prayer. Additionally, a journal acts as a permanent reminder of God's activity and faithfulness in your life. To start journaling, simply grab a notebook or an electronic device. Document your prayers, note how God answered them, and express your deepest feelings. Reflect on what God is teaching you through His Word and your life circumstances. This practice can foster spiritual growth by keeping you purposeful and accountable.

Prayerful Anticipation

Incorporating prayer into your periods of waiting transforms the experience from one of passive inactivity to one of active engagement with God. Prayerful anticipation involves praying not just for the object of your wait but also for the patience and faith to endure the waiting period itself. Use this time to build a deeper reliance on God. Pray for wisdom, understanding, and peace. Remember that David frequently moved from sorrow or anxiety to joy and trust by reminding himself of God's past deeds and promises (The Spiritual Discipline of Journaling | Christian Library, 2014). By incorporating these elements into your prayers, you align your heart with God's timing and plans.

Setting Mini-Goals

Waiting doesn't mean putting your life on hold. Setting mini-goals can help you focus on spiritual growth during this period. These goals should be achievable and directly related to your spiritual journey. Maybe it's committing to daily Scripture reading, enhancing your prayer life, or serving in a ministry. Write these goals down in your waiting journal and track your progress. This not only keeps you engaged but also helps you see tangible evidence of growth, even when you're still waiting for larger prayers to be answered.

Now, let's take a breather and delve deeper into each point, offering more examples and concrete steps to ensure these practices become a natural part of your spiritual life.

Mindfulness Techniques

To dive deeper into practicing mindfulness, consider setting aside specific times of day to meditate on Scripture. Start your morning with a short devotional reading and spend five minutes reflecting on its meaning. During the day, take mindful moments—pausing before meals, during breaks, or at bedtime—to check in with God. Ask questions like, "What are You teaching me in this moment?" or "How can I serve others while I wait?" These brief yet intentional pauses can recalibrate your focus, making your wait a fruitful period of spiritual awareness.

Journaling Methods

For those new to journaling, the process may seem intimidating. Here's a straightforward method: Begin each journal entry with a date and a brief summary of your day. Follow with any Scriptures that stood out to you and why they resonated. Then write down your prayers—both requests and thanksgivings. Finally, end with reflections on what you're learning about patience and God's faithfulness. Over time, patterns may emerge that highlight areas where God is actively working in your life, providing encouragement during extended waiting periods.

Integrating Prayer

To make prayerful anticipation a consistent practice, try integrating it into your daily routine. Morning prayers could focus on surrendering your anxieties about waiting, asking God to shape your character through the process. Lunchtime prayers might involve thanking God for small blessings observed throughout the day. Evening prayers could concentrate on reviewing your day, seeking forgiveness, and expressing gratitude. Using the Psalms as a guide can also be helpful. Notice how David's prayers often started in despair but ended in praise. Emulate this pattern in your own prayers to cultivate a hopeful and trusting attitude.

Achieving Mini-Goals

Breaking down your spiritual growth into mini-goals can make the waiting period less daunting and more productive. If one of your goals is to improve your Bible study habits, start with something manageable, like reading one chapter of Proverbs daily. If another goal is community service, begin with small acts of kindness like volunteering once a month at a local shelter. Keep a dedicated section in your journal for these goals, noting your progress and reflecting on how achieving them impacts your faith journey. Celebrate these small victories as milestones that bring you closer to God.

Lastly, it's essential to recognize that waiting can be a deeply personal experience, differing greatly from one individual to another. While these guidelines provide a structured approach, remain open to how God uniquely leads you during your waiting periods. Be gentle with yourself, and remember that spiritual growth often happens in the hidden, quiet moments. Waiting may seem like a detour, but it's an integral part of the journey—one that prepares you for future peaks and valleys of faith.

Summary and Reflections

In this chapter, we've delved into the art and importance of waiting on God, uncovering its deeper spiritual implications. We've journeyed through the difference between passive and active waiting, like comparing a couch potato to an eager gardener. The biblical examples of Abraham and Moses have shown us that although waiting can feel like you're stuck in a slow-motion movie, it's actually a vital period where patience and faith bloom. We learned that while the world is all about quick fixes and fast lanes, God's timeline offers lessons in humility and trust.

As we wrap up our exploration, remember that waiting on God isn't just a test of endurance but a time for growth. Embracing mindfulness, journaling, prayerful anticipation, and setting mini-goals can transform your wait from a tedious pause into a fruitful adventure. So next time you feel like you're staring at the spinning wheel of life's loading screen, take heart. God's got impeccable timing, even when it feels like He's using dial-up.

Chapter Two

Trusting in Unseen Promises

Trusting in unseen promises is like betting on a surprise party being thrown by someone who's never missed an occasion. You've marked the date, but the balloons and confetti are all hypothetical until you walk into that room. This chapter dives headfirst into the art of maintaining rock-solid faith during those pesky waiting periods when God's promises seem like whispers in the wind. Imagine knowing that the big reveal is coming but having no clue when or how it will happen. It's like ordering a mystery box online and waiting for the doorbell to ring.

In this chapter, we'll flip through the pages of some old-school examples of faith that make waiting look like an extreme sport. We'll see Noah hammer away at an ark despite folks thinking he's gone off the deep end. Then, there's Moses leading an impromptu desert expedition that lasts four decades—imagine trying to keep everyone happy without Wi-Fi! We also have Anna, who practically lived at the temple praying her heart out until her patience was rewarded. And let's not forget Job, whose middle name might as well be "Endurance." Through these tales, we'll explore how to cultivate that unshakeable belief in God's perfect timing and unfailing promises, even when it feels like you're holding onto a noisemaker waiting for the stroke of midnight.

Biblical Examples of Faith in Waiting

Imagine a situation where you're asked to do something that seems utterly preposterous. That's precisely the scenario Noah found himself in, yet his faith remained steadfast. God instructed him to build an enormous ark because a flood was coming—a concept so foreign at the time that it was laughable. Rain? What's that? Water falling from the sky? Absurd! Nevertheless, Noah obeyed without delay or second-guessing, rolling up his sleeves and getting to work.

Noah's proactive obedience under uncertainty showcases tough, enduring faith. For 120 years, he pounded nails into wood, crafting a vessel more massive than any football stadium you've ever seen. Day after day, year after year, the ark took shape while people around him mocked and questioned his sanity. However, Noah's commitment never wavered—he trusted beyond what his eyes could see and continued building until the ark was complete. Imagine waking up every morning and looking at a half-done ship in your backyard with neighbors whispering behind your back, "Is he lost his marbles?" Yet, Noah persisted, driven by his belief in God's promise of salvation through the ark. His faith wasn't just a feeling; it was active and visible. He believed deeply, and he acted on that belief, illustrating that true faith often includes doing something radical (Village Bible Church, 2018).

Let's shift gears and talk about Moses and the Israelites. Picture leading a whole nation—a multitude as large as a modern city—through a desert for 40 years. We're not talking about a weekend camping trip with some hiccups. This is four decades of wandering with limited food and water resources. Moses' journey underscores reliance on divine guidance and sustenance, shaping the Israelites' identity and purpose.

From manna falling daily from heaven (talk about miraculous home delivery!) to water springing from rocks, their time in the wilderness was peppered with continuous reminders that God provided exactly what they needed, exactly when they needed it. Each step in their prolonged trek taught them patience and trust. They learned to lean not on their understanding but on God's provision and promises. Dependence on divine guidance became paramount, like using Google Maps but trusting it way more for life-death decisions, ensuring the journey wasn't just about reaching the Promised Land but about the transformation occurring along the way.

Now, picture Anna the Prophetess. She's the spiritual marathoner of her day, hanging out in the temple like it's her second home, praying day and night. Why? Because she had one burning desire: to see the Messiah. Imagine spending years, decades even, on your knees in persistent prayer and fasting. That's what Anna did—she showed up, day in and day out, waiting for the fulfillment of a promise she knew deep down would come.

What's inspiring here is not just her patience but her relentless devotion despite the wait. Finally, when baby Jesus made his temple debut, Anna's joy knew no bounds. In that moment, all her years of tireless anticipation culminated in pure elation. Her story highlights that while waiting can be exasperating, the arrival of God's promises brings immeasurable joy worth every second of the wait. It teaches us that perseverance in prayer and devotion can lead to encounters with divine moments that make all the waiting worthwhile.

Lastly, let's discuss Job, the poster child for enduring hardship with unyielding faith. If there were an award for the person who faced the most trials without breaking, Job would probably have a trophy shelf full of them. Stripped of wealth, health, and family, you'd think Job might throw in the towel. But instead, he chose to trust God's bigger plan even when life seemed unbearably bleak.

Through his immense suffering, Job insisted that God's promises were real. Think of it like this—his friends were like, "Curse God and give up!" But Job held firm, believing deeper blessings awaited him post-trial. And guess what? He was right! After the whirlwind of tests, God restored everything to Job tenfold, proving that unimaginable hardships can sometimes pave the way for unparalleled blessings. Job's unwavering faith serves as a beacon for those facing their own storms, suggesting the value of hanging on even when it's dark, and trusting that light is just around the corner.

So there you have it—four prime examples of robust faith in times of waiting. We've seen Noah swing his hammer in unwavering obedience, Moses and the Israelites wander with trust, Anna persistently pray until her joy was full, and Job endure with hope through unimaginable trials. These narratives aren't just ancient stories; they are living testimonies to the power of faith and the assurance of God's promises.

Identifying and Overcoming Doubt

Understanding doubts as part of the journey during waiting periods can be an unsettling experience. It's natural to question and feel uncertain when the future is cloudy and promises seem delayed. Yet, these doubts shouldn't be seen as failures or weaknesses but rather as integral aspects of our faith journey. Acknowledging and addressing doubt is pivotal; it fosters personal and spiritual growth, turning these moments of uncertainty into opportunities for deeper faith.

Consider doubt as a stepping stone rather than a stumbling block. When you find yourself wrestling with questions about God's timing or His plans, view this as a chance to grow closer to Him. These moments of vulnerability can lead to more significant reliance on God. Think of doubt like a workout for your spiritual muscles; it may be uncomfortable, but it ultimately strengthens your faith. Instead of shying away from these feelings, embrace them and use them as a lens to examine your faith more closely.

Implementing practical faith exercises is crucial in combating doubt and staying focused on God's goodness. Daily affirmations are a powerful tool. Start each day by speaking positive truths over your life, such as "I trust in God's perfect timing" or "His promises are unfailing." This practice helps rewire your mind to focus on positivity and trust rather than uncertainty and fear.

Prayer is another vital exercise. Make time every day to communicate with God. Prayer doesn't have to be formal; think of it as a heart-to-heart conversation with a friend. In these quiet moments, express your fears and doubts to God; ask Him for strength and clarity. Bearing your soul in prayer can provide peace and reassurance beyond understanding.

Gratitude, too, plays a fundamental role. Actively listing things you're thankful for redirects your attention from what you lack to the abundance already present in your life. Even during difficult waiting periods, focusing on gratitude helps highlight God's continuous provision and blessings, fostering a hopeful perspective.

Utilizing scripture against doubt is another effective strategy. The Bible is rich with verses that speak to God's unwavering promises. Identifying and reflecting on these verses can offer comfort and reinforce trust during shaky times. For instance, Jeremiah 29:11 says, "For I know the plans I have for you," declares the Lord, "plans to prosper you and not to harm you, plans to give you hope and a future." Reflecting on this promise can help anchor your trust in God's plans, even when they aren't immediately clear.

Think of scripture as a spiritual toolkit, providing the necessary tools to combat doubt. Spend time regularly reading and meditating on verses that resonate with your current situation. Write them down, carry them with you, or post them where you'll see them often. Let these scriptures serve as a constant reminder of God's faithfulness.

Seeking mentorship or counsel also offers valuable support in navigating doubts through a lens of faith. Engaging with spiritual mentors provides fresh perspectives and accountability. These individuals can offer wisdom born from their own experiences and guide you through the murkiness of your doubts.

Mentorship isn't just about receiving advice; it's about building a relationship rooted in mutual trust and respect. Your mentor can help you see your situation from a different angle, offering insights you might have overlooked. They can pray with you, provide encouragement, and hold you accountable to your faith practices, making the journey less daunting.

Moreover, participating in group counseling or joining a faith-based community group can bolster your efforts to overcome doubt. Surrounding yourself with a supportive community creates a network of individuals who understand and share similar experiences. They can walk alongside you, offering empathy and solidarity.

During one-on-one or group sessions, be open about your struggles and listen actively to others' stories. Often, hearing how someone else navigated their doubts can inspire and motivate you to persevere. Remember, you are not alone; many have walked this path before and come out stronger on the other side.

Building Trust Through Prayer and Scripture

Cultivating trust in God during waiting periods can often feel like trying to see through a foggy window. You know there's something beautiful outside, but it's hard to make out the details. This is where prayer comes in as your defogger, gradually clearing the haze.

Regular communication with God transforms waiting from passive idleness into purposeful engagement. Think of prayer as your daily check-in with God, like catching up over coffee with a dear friend who always has your best interests at heart. When you pray, you're not just sending out wishful thinking into the ether; you are actively participating in God's timeline for your life. It's through these conversations that you begin to realize that His timing—no matter how inscrutable—is perfect.

One practical step to deepen this practice is to set aside specific times each day for prayer. Whether it's first thing in the morning, during a lunch break, or right before bed, having designated prayer times can help transform sporadic communication into a disciplined habit. Make a cozy nook where you feel comfortable and focused, maybe light a candle or have some calming music in the background. The key is consistency which turns routine into ritual, making the time spent waiting less about impatience and more about engaging purposefully with God's plan.

Integrating scripture readings with prayer is another vital practice. It's like pairing your favorite meal with the perfect wine; each enhances the other. By delving into scripture, you uncover truths and promises that provide encouragement and strength. Readers, grab your Bibles! Look for passages that speak to trusting God's timing, such as Jeremiah 29:11, "For I know the plans I have for you," declares the Lord, "plans to prosper you and not to harm you, plans to give you hope and a future." Meditating on these verses within your prayers makes the message resonate on a deeper level, turning abstract ideas into personal affirmations of faith.

For those keen on maximizing their spiritual growth, journaling prayers and reflections offers an insightful tool. Writing down your conversations with God helps you track your journey and recognize patterns of His faithfulness. Remember those days when you felt like nothing was happening? Flip back a few pages, and you'll likely find instances where God showed up in unexpected ways. Journaling acts as both a record and a reminder—a tangible manifestation of God's ongoing work in your life.

Get a notebook dedicated to this purpose. Start by jotting down your daily prayers, hopes, fears, and any scriptures that stood out to you during your reading. Over time, you'll build a collection of experiences that highlight God's consistent presence and guidance. Imagine flipping through these pages years from now and seeing all the ways God answered your prayers—it's like finding hidden treasures in your own backyard!

Accountability partnerships add yet another layer of support and encouragement. Finding a prayer partner or joining a prayer group allows you to share the experience of waiting on God with others. It's like running a marathon; having someone by your side cheering you on can make all the difference. These partnerships create a space for shared vulnerability, collective prayer, and mutual encouragement. Knowing there's someone else interceding for you provides an added sense of hope and unity.

Consider reaching out to a close friend or someone you respect spiritually and propose meeting once a week for prayer. Share your struggles, celebrate your victories, and most importantly, pray for one another. The act of vocalizing your needs and hearing someone else lift them up in prayer fosters a powerful connection—not just with each other, but with God.

Incorporating these practices into your life doesn't require grandiose changes. It's about small, consistent steps that cumulatively cultivate a deep-seated trust in God. Regular prayer transforms waiting into purposeful engagement, anchoring you firmly in reliance on His timing. Incorporating scripture enriches your faith, filling your mind with divine truths. Journaling serves as a reflective tool, helping you see God's faithful hand even when current circumstances seem bleak.

Lastly, accountability partnerships offer communal support, ensuring you're not navigating this journey alone.

Bringing It All Together

Faith and trust in God's timing might seem like a tall order when life's challenges have us feeling like extras in a never-ending drama series. Yet, the stories of Noah, Moses, Anna, and Job show us that faith isn't just about waiting passively but engaging actively. Whether it's Noah hammering away at an ark while everyone thought he was one fry short of a Happy Meal, or Moses leading a grumbling crowd through an endless sand pit, their journeys remind us that God's promises arrive at precisely the right moment. These stories flip our perspective on waiting, transforming it into an adventure filled with growth, trust, and the eventual joy that comes with seeing God's hand at work.

As you navigate your own waiting periods, remember that doubt isn't a sign of weak faith; it's a stepping stone to deeper trust. Embrace those "What-am-I-doing?" moments as opportunities for growth. Use prayer, scripture, gratitude, and mentorship as your toolkit to build resilience. Treat prayer like catching up with a friend over coffee—consistent and comforting. Lean on scriptures for strength and let journaling capture your spiritual milestones. And don't forget the power of community; having someone cheer you on can make all the difference. With these practices, waiting doesn't have to be a frustrating pause but a rich season of transformation and anticipation for what's to come.

Chapter Three

The Role of Patience

P atience is often rumored to be a virtue, but if you've ever been stuck in an endless traffic jam or on hold with customer service for what feels like eternity, you might have your doubts. It's easy to think of patience as simply waiting around doing nothing, but this chapter will introduce you to a much richer, more dynamic view of patience that's far from boring. Patience isn't just sitting there twiddling your thumbs and counting ceiling tiles. In fact, true patience involves actively engaging with life's unpredictable moments, transforming them into opportunities for growth and reflection. And let's be honest, we could all use a little help in the patience department—especially when the Wi-Fi goes down during our favorite show!

In this chapter, we'll dive deep into the essence of patience and how it's deeply rooted in Christian faith. You'll discover how this seemingly passive quality can actually become a powerful tool for spiritual growth and maturity. We'll break down biblical examples, actionable exercises, and real-life applications to build patience in various aspects of your busy life. From keeping calm during minor daily irritations like slow-moving grocery lines to maintaining grace and understanding amid significant challenges, you'll learn practical methods to cultivate patience. So get ready to transform those frustrating moments into stepping stones for a more fulfilling and spiritually enriched life.

Understanding Patience as a Virtue

Patience, often misunderstood as mere waiting, is a dynamic virtue that fosters spiritual growth and strengthens faith. It's more than just idly biding our time; it's an active engagement with our surroundings and circumstances, reflecting the profound character of God Himself. As a fruit of the Spirit, patience is deeply embedded in Scripture and recognized as an enduring quality essential for a faithful Christian life.

In the biblical context, patience is closely tied to long-suffering, a concept that extends beyond simple endurance. Long-suffering reflects a depth and significance that urges believers to pursue this virtue actively. This is particularly evident in passages like Galatians 5:22-23, where patience is listed among the fruits of the Spirit, underscoring its importance in a believer's life (The Fruit of Patience, 2024). The idea here isn't just to endure but to do so with grace and understanding, knowing that our trials have a purpose and ultimately lead to spiritual maturity.

Everyday situations constantly test our patience, whether it's dealing with traffic jams, waiting for important news, or navigating challenging relationships. These moments are more than just inconveniences; they act as mirrors reflecting our character and spiritual maturity. It's in these testing times that we truly see how deeply patience is ingrained in us. For instance, standing in a long line at the grocery store might reveal our impulse to grumble or complain, showcasing areas where we need to grow. By consciously applying patience in such situations, we gradually build resilience and demonstrate a steady, unwavering faith.

Moreover, demonstrating patience can serve as a powerful testimony to non-believers. In a world driven by instant gratification, the ability to patiently endure challenges without resentment or frustration stands out. It bridges understanding within the community and fosters connections that can lead others to explore the faith. Imagine someone observing a Christian enduring a difficult situation with calm and grace; it speaks volumes about the transformative power of faith and can inspire curiosity and respect from those who may not share the same beliefs.

One striking example of biblical patience is found in the story of Job. Despite immense suffering and loss, Job's faith never wavered. He famously declared, "Though he slay me, yet will I hope in him" (Job 13:15). Job's perseverance is a testament to the depth of his faith and his understanding of God's character. His story reminds us that patience isn't passive but an active stance fueled by trust in God's timing and promises.

Another reflection of patience as an enduring quality is seen in the nature of God's patience with humanity. God's patience is long but not infinite, reminding believers of the balance between divine mercy and justice. God's character of being slow to anger and quick to be merciful offers a model for our behavior. This aspect of patience is especially relevant when dealing with personal injury or injustice. Unlike the immediacy we crave in vindication, God's justice operates on His perfect timeline, teaching us to trust in His plan rather than rushing for our own resolution.

The everyday tests of patience aren't limited to grand gestures or significant events; they manifest in subtle forms like parenting, work, and even social interactions. For instance, a parent might find their patience tested by a rebellious teenager. Rather than responding with frustration, approaching the situation with calm and understanding can transform the experience into a lesson in patience for both the parent and the child. Similarly, in a work environment, dealing with a challenging colleague can either lead to conflict or become an opportunity to practice and exhibit patience, thereby setting a positive example for others.

Biblical figures such as Abraham and Sarah also underscore the virtue of patience. Their long wait for the promised child, Isaac, showcases a blend of human frailty and divine faithfulness. Despite moments of doubt and impatience, their story culminates in the fulfillment of God's promise, reinforcing the belief that patience rooted in faith is always rewarded in due time.

Furthermore, patience plays a crucial role in cultivating other virtues like forgiveness, humility, and love. When we exercise patience, especially in relationships, it opens the door for forgiveness. Take, for instance, a scenario where a friend betrays our trust. Instead of immediately severing the relationship, choosing to approach the situation with patience allows space for dialogue, understanding, and ultimately, forgiveness. This process not only heals wounds but also deepens the bond, enriching our spiritual journey.

Humility also thrives in the soil of patience. Recognizing that we aren't always in control and accepting delays or setbacks with a humble heart aligns us closer to God's purpose. It shifts our perspective from self-centeredness to a broader understanding of our place in God's plan. For example, aspiring for a promotion at work but facing repeated delays can be disheartening. However, viewing this period as God's way of preparing us for greater responsibility fosters humility and strengthens our faith.

Love, the greatest of all virtues, is intricately connected with patience. In 1 Corinthians 13, Paul describes love as patient and kind. Patience, in this context, is not just about tolerating others but actively seeking their good despite challenges or disappointments. A loving relationship, whether romantic, familial, or platonic, flourishes when nurtured with patience. It means giving others time to grow, understanding their flaws, and supporting them without rushing or pressuring.

Practical Exercises to Develop Patience

Cultivating patience can sometimes feel like trying to catch a greased pig—slippery, elusive, and downright frustrating. However, imbedding patience into our daily lives is not only possible but also incredibly beneficial for both our spiritual growth and mental well-being. In this section, we will discuss several actionable techniques that can help you develop patience seamlessly.

First and foremost, incorporating mindfulness and meditation practices into your routine can significantly enhance your ability to remain patient. These practices serve as an anchor, helping you stay aware of your thoughts and feelings without getting carried away by them. When you're mindful, you observe your frustrations rather than react to them immediately. This heightened awareness fosters a sense of inner calm, which naturally lends itself to a more patient disposition. For instance, during moments of agitation, take a few minutes to close your eyes, breathe deeply, and center yourself. Eventually, this habit becomes second nature, and you'll find that your patience has improved considerably. Taking the time to be mindful and meditate regularly enhances emotional balance and reduces stress, making it easier to remain patient in challenging situations (Eisler, 2018).

Next up is aligning your expectations with reality. Often, impatience stems from a mismatch between what we expect and what actually happens. It's easy to get frustrated when life doesn't go according to plan. By setting realistic expectations, you can prevent such frustration and maintain a sense of peace even during waiting periods. This approach involves understanding that some things are beyond your control and that waiting is a part of life. Aligning expectations with reality encourages you to communicate with God continuously, seeking His guidance and trusting in His timing. This act of surrender helps mitigate disappointment and fosters an ongoing dialogue with the Divine, strengthening your faith in the process.

Another incredibly effective technique for cultivating patience is journaling. Engage in the practice of writing down your experiences and reflections related to waiting and patience. Journaling allows you to track your progress, identify patterns, and visualize growth over time. It also serves as a tool for fostering gratitude. When you document the lessons learned through periods of waiting, you begin to appreciate the journey rather than just focusing on the outcome. Additionally, journaling can provide a much-needed outlet for venting frustrations and acknowledging small victories, thereby reinforcing your resolve to practice patience consistently. Keeping a regular journal entry about how you handled specific scenarios provides tangible evidence of your growth, motivating you to continue the practice.

Scripture is another powerful resource for cultivating patience. Select, memorize, and use biblical verses in your prayers to remind yourself of God's promises and to draw strength during tough times. Verses like "But they who wait for the Lord shall renew their strength; they shall mount up with wings like eagles; they shall run and not be weary; they shall walk and not faint" (Isaiah 40:31) serve as constant reminders of the virtue of patience. They offer encouragement and reassurance, especially when you're feeling overwhelmed. Integrating these verses into your daily prayers helps keep you grounded and fortifies your spirit, making it easier to remain patient. Reciting scripture during moments of impatience acts as a spiritual balm, soothing anxiety and replacing it with divine peace (pearman, 2019).

Mindfulness and meditation, setting realistic expectations, journaling, and utilizing scripture are more than mere techniques; they form a holistic approach to integrating patience into your life. Each method complements the others, creating a robust framework for enduring life's trials with grace and composure. Practicing these methods consistently turns patience from a fleeting aspiration into a permanent virtue embedded in your character.

As we delve deeper into these techniques, let's explore some real-life applications. Consider a situation where you're stuck in a seemingly endless traffic jam. Instead of fuming and honking, pause and breathe deeply. Realize that your impatience won't clear the road any faster. Use this downtime to practice mindfulness—observe your surroundings, listen to calming music, or even recite a favorite scripture. This simple shift in perspective can transform a potential stressor into a moment of tranquility.

Similarly, think about the times when you're eager for a career breakthrough that seems to be taking forever. Align your expectations with reality by recognizing that achievements often require persistent effort and time. In your journal, document the steps you've taken towards your goal and the progress you've made, no matter how small. Reflecting on this can give you a sense of accomplishment and motivate you to keep going.

Incorporate scripture readings into your morning or evening routines. Start your day with a verse like Psalm 46:10, "Be still, and know that I am God," to set a patient tone for the day ahead. During the evening, review your journal entries and thank God for the lessons learned through the day's challenges, big or small.

The Link Between Patience and Spiritual Maturity

Growing in patience is deeply intertwined with overall spiritual development and maturity. In the Christian faith, the ability to remain patient during trials is a clear marker of spiritual maturity, often leading to the cultivation of other vital virtues like forgiveness, humility, and love.

Spiritual maturity is frequently showcased through one's ability to remain calm and composed in the face of adversity. It's during tough times that patience becomes most valuable. For instance, imagine someone wrongs you at work. Instead of reacting impulsively, you take a deep breath, reflect on the situation, and choose to forgive the person. This act of patience can lead to improved relationships and personal growth. Forgiveness, as an extension of patience, allows believers to let go of grudges and embrace peace, showcasing a mature and loving spirit.

Moreover, patience fosters humility. When faced with setbacks or delays, we are reminded of our limitations and dependence on God. Recognizing that we do not control everything humbles us, teaching us to rely on God's timing rather than our own. This humility paves the way for love, as it positions us to put others' needs before our own. In waiting patiently for others, we learn to love more genuinely, honoring them above ourselves.

Hardships are inevitable, but coveting patience during these times builds resilience and steadfastness. Think about an athlete training for a marathon. The journey is grueling, filled with moments of doubt and physical pain. Yet, by enduring these hardships patiently, the athlete becomes stronger and more determined. Similarly, when life's challenges test our patience, responding with grace strengthens our resolve and equips us to handle future difficulties with greater ease.

Incorporating patience in our daily lives gradually transforms us, enabling us to respond to adversities with grace rather than frustration. Consider the case of losing a job. It's easy to become disheartened, but embracing patience allows you to seek new opportunities with hope and determination rather than despair. This resilience not only benefits you but also serves as an inspiration to those around you.

Engaging in a community of support fosters an environment where patience can be cultivated together and strengthens bonds of faith. Picture a church group that meets weekly to share struggles and victories. Such a community provides a safe space for individuals to express their frustrations and receive encouragement. When you see others practicing patience and hear their stories of perseverance, it motivates you to cultivate the same virtue. Additionally, supporting each other through prayer and shared experiences creates a strong sense of camaraderie and mutual faith, making the journey towards spiritual maturity more manageable.

Communities play a crucial role in shaping our behaviors and attitudes. For instance, being part of a Bible study group allows you to witness firsthand how others exercise patience amid trials. These observations serve as practical lessons, demonstrating that patience is achievable and worthwhile. Moreover, community support offers accountability, gently reminding you to stay patient even when it's challenging.

A long-term perspective encourages understanding of God's timing and plans, emphasizing hope amidst waiting and fostering a future-oriented mindset. Often, our impatience stems from focusing too much on immediate desires rather than trusting in God's perfect timing. By adopting a long-term perspective, we shift our focus from present discomfort to future promises.

Imagine planting a seed. It takes time for it to sprout and grow into a flourishing plant. The process requires patience, but the end result is rewarding. Similarly, viewing life's challenges through a long-term lens allows us to embrace the waiting period, knowing that God has a purpose and plan for everything. This perspective helps us endure present trials with hope and faith, looking forward to the fulfillment of God's promises.

Emphasizing a future-oriented mindset helps manage expectations and reduces frustration. When we trust that God's timing is impeccable, we are less likely to feel anxious or rushed. This trust not only provides inner peace but also strengthens our faith, reinforcing the belief that all things work together for good in due time (Spiritual Growth Definition, Importance, Characteristics and Examples, n.d.).

Patience also nurtures hope. As we wait for God's plans to unfold, our anticipation becomes rooted in hope, a confident expectation of what lies ahead. This hope sustains us through difficult seasons, reminding us that our current struggles are temporary and that God's promises are worth the wait. It fuels our perseverance, urging us to keep going despite the challenges.

Insights and Implications

Patience, as we've explored here, isn't just sitting around twiddling our thumbs waiting for something to happen. It's an active virtue that shapes our character and deepens our faith. By applying patience in everyday situations—like traffic jams or workplace challenges—we not only build resilience but also act as living testimonies to others. Imagine handling a frustrating scenario with calm and grace; it not only feels better but also showcases the transformative power of faith.

Practicing patience through mindfulness, realistic expectations, journaling, and scripture can make this elusive virtue more tangible. Think of these methods as tools in your spiritual toolkit, ready to help when impatience sneaks up. Whether you're stuck in a long line or awaiting life-altering news, these habits enable you to remain grounded. And remember, each moment of patience is a small victory, a step toward greater spiritual maturity and a testament to your unwavering trust in God's perfect timing.

Chapter Four

Navigating Emotional Challenges

D ealing with the emotional whirlwind of waiting can be as fun as watching paint dry while standing on one leg. Whether you're eagerly counting down days until a job offer or biting your nails for medical results, it's easy to let anxiety take over. This chapter is all about taming that inner chaos monster. We're diving into practical and effective tools to manage those nail-biting moments without tearing your hair out – because let's face it, you need that mane for dramatic hair flips when good news arrives.

Ready to turn the tables on anxiety and frustration? We'll explore a variety of techniques to help you stay sane during the agonizing wait. From mindfulness practices that make you feel like a Zen master to breath prayers that bring serenity faster than a cup of chamomile tea, we've got you covered. You'll also discover the power of scriptural affirmations to fortify your mind and physical activities to kick those jittery nerves to the curb. Stick with us, and you'll learn how to flip the script on anxious waiting and make peace and assurance your trusty companions.

Techniques for Managing Anxiety

In today's fast-paced world, waiting periods can be riddled with anxiety and frustration. Whether you're awaiting job applications, medical results, or personal milestones, the uncertainty can easily overshadow your peace of mind. This part of our journey aims to equip you with practical strategies to alleviate anxiety during these times. With the right approaches, you can navigate these waiting periods with a sense of peace and assurance.

First up, let's delve into mindfulness practices. Mindfulness is all about being present in the moment, fully engaging with what you're doing or experiencing. When we are riddled with anxiety, our minds often spiral into "what if" scenarios, projecting fears about an uncertain future. Here's where mindfulness steps in like a faithful friend, gently pulling us back to the here and now. Try this: The next time you're feeling anxious, take a moment to notice your surroundings. What can you see? Hear? Smell? Touch? Taste? Pay close attention to these details without judgment. It could be the shade of blue on a wall, the hum of your refrigerator, or the warmth of a cup of tea in your hands. Grounding yourself in the present moment can drastically reduce anxiety levels. As Victoria from the National Brain Tumor Society notes, "Noticing things in the present moment is what mindfulness is in a nutshell" (Managing Scanxiety: 5 Ways to Reduce Scan-Related Anxiety through Self-Care - National Brain Tumor Society, 2023).

Next, let's talk about breath prayer techniques. This is a simple yet powerful method to calm your spirit and focus your thoughts. Breath prayers are short, meaningful phrases synchronized with your breathing pattern. For instance, as you inhale, you might think, "God is here." As you exhale, you might say, "I am at peace." This practice not only helps center your mind but also makes space for spiritual connection. The rhythmic nature of breath prayers allows you to tap into a calming ritual anytime, anywhere. Imagine standing in line at the grocery store or waiting in a doctor's office; instead of spiraling into worry, you can engage in breath prayer, turning idle moments into sanctuaries of peace.

Now, onto scriptural affirmations. Words have power, and repeating affirmations based on scripture can be a game-changer for mental resilience. Consider affirmations like, "The Lord is my shepherd; I shall not want" (Psalm 23:1) or "I can do all things through Christ who strengthens me" (Philippians 4:13). Repeating these verses, either mentally or aloud, can reinforce your faith and reduce feelings of helplessness. Write them down on sticky notes and place them where you'll see them frequently—your bathroom mirror, your car dashboard, or even your journal. By embedding these affirmations into your daily routine, you create a mental fortress that guards against anxiety and nurtures inner strength.

Last but not least, let's touch on the importance of physical activity. When anxiety builds up, it often manifests physically—tight shoulders, a churning stomach, shallow breaths. Engaging in regular physical exercise can help release this built-up tension, acting as a natural antidote to stress. You don't have to become a marathon runner or a yoga guru overnight. Even small, consistent activities like walking your dog, dancing around your living room, or tending to your garden can make a significant difference. Physical activity boosts the production of endorphins, the body's natural mood lifters, helping to create a sense of well-being. Moreover, incorporating a mindfulness element into physical activity, such as mindful walking or stretching, can amplify its stress-relieving benefits. Picture yourself taking a walk in a park, feeling the ground beneath your feet, the rustle of leaves in the wind, and the sun warming your face. Each step becomes a meditative act, grounding you further into the peaceful present.

Incorporating these strategies into your daily life doesn't require drastic changes—all it takes is a commitment to making small, intentional shifts. By introducing mindfulness practices, you learn to anchor yourself in the present, cutting off anxiety at its roots. Through breath prayer techniques, you find a way to turn everyday moments into opportunities for spiritual connection and peace. Scriptural affirmations fortify your mind with powerful truths, building resilience against emotional disturbances. And lastly, by embracing physical activity, you give your body a constructive outlet to dispel tension and boost overall well-being.

Waiting will always be a part of life. But with these tools, you can transform periods of uncertainty into opportunities for growth and serenity. Remember, it's not about completely eradicating anxiety but rather learning how to manage it effectively. So the next time you're caught in the web of waiting, reach into your toolkit and draw upon the power of mindfulness, breath prayers, scriptural affirmations, and physical activity. You'll find that peace and assurance aren't distant dreams but companions you can call upon whenever you need them most.

Healthy Ways to Cope with Frustration

Emotions can run high during prolonged waiting periods, and one of the most challenging feelings to navigate is frustration. To help readers manage these emotions effectively, this subpoint presents practical coping mechanisms designed to reduce frustration and promote emotional well-being. Here are some strategies to explore:

Journaling for Clarity

Journaling can be a powerful tool for processing frustration. It allows you to put your emotions on paper, making them more tangible and easier to understand. When you journal, there's no need for perfect grammar or spelling; it's about expressing your thoughts and feelings freely. You might start by writing down what's bothering you, then move on to how it makes you feel. This process helps clarify the root causes of your frustration and identifies patterns in your emotional responses.

To make journaling even more effective, consider setting aside a specific time each day to write. Consistency can turn journaling into a regular habit, providing ongoing benefits. Some people find it helpful to use prompts like "What frustrated me today?" or "How did I react to a challenging situation?" These questions can guide your writing and deepen your insights.

Setting Realistic Expectations

Setting realistic expectations is crucial during waiting periods. Often, frustration stems from unmet expectations, so adjusting your goals can alleviate much of this tension. Start by assessing the situation objectively. Ask yourself what you can reasonably achieve within a given timeframe. Break larger tasks into smaller, more manageable steps, and set deadlines for each one.

It's also essential to remain flexible. Understand that delays and unexpected changes can happen, and being prepared for these possibilities can reduce frustration. If you find yourself feeling overwhelmed, take a step back and reconsider your goals. Are they still attainable, or do they need to be adjusted? Regularly reviewing and updating your expectations ensures they remain realistic and achievable.

Moreover, communicating your expectations with others involved in the process can prevent misunderstandings and shared frustrations. Open dialogue helps align everyone's goals and timelines, creating a more cohesive and supportive environment.

Creative Outlets

Channeling frustration into creative activities can be incredibly therapeutic. Whether it's painting, writing, gardening, or playing an instrument, engaging in a hobby allows you to express your emotions constructively. Creativity provides a distraction and offers a different perspective on your situation, which can change how you perceive and deal with frustration.

For example, if you're waiting for a job offer and feeling frustrated by the lack of response, you might take up a new hobby or return to one you love. Creating something tangible, like a painting or a piece of music, can give you a sense of accomplishment and progress, which counteracts feelings of stagnation.

Even simple activities like doodling or crafting can serve as emotional outlets. The act of creation requires focus and attention, which can shift your mind away from frustrating thoughts. Plus, the end product of your creative work can provide a sense of pride and satisfaction, lifting your overall mood.

Seeking Guidance from Mentors

During frustrating times, reaching out to mentors or trusted friends can offer invaluable support. Mentors, particularly those with more experience, can provide perspective and advice that you might not have considered. They can also share their own experiences of navigating similar situations, which can be both comforting and instructive.

Don't hesitate to ask for guidance. It shows strength and a willingness to grow. A mentor can help you see the bigger picture and remind you of your long-term goals, which can be motivating when you're feeling stuck. They might also suggest alternative approaches to your challenges, offering new strategies to overcome obstacles.

If you're not sure where to find a mentor, consider joining professional organizations or community groups related to your interests. These environments often foster mentorship relationships and provide opportunities to connect with individuals who can guide you through tough times.

Summary

The Role of Community in Emotional Support

Navigating the emotional roller coaster of waiting can be an isolating experience. However, community and shared experiences play vital roles in providing much-needed support. This subpoint will explore how forming support groups, engaging in church communities, sharing stories, and creating a culture of offering and requesting help can bring stability during trying times.

Forming Support GroupsWhen it comes to battling anxiety and frustration during prolonged waiting periods, one of the most effective strategies is becoming part of a support group. These groups act as lifeboats, offering a safe space to share emotions, experiences, and coping mechanisms. Being surrounded by individuals who are going through similar situations can greatly reduce feelings of loneliness and despair. Support groups provide a platform for venting feelings, seeking advice, and even celebrating small victories along the journey.

To form a successful support group, start by reaching out to friends or acquaintances who might be experiencing similar waits. Even if your immediate circle doesn't include such individuals, expanding your search online can yield fruitful connections. Online forums, social media groups, and local community centers often host support groups focusing on specific issues.

Once connected, schedule regular meetings either in-person or virtually. The consistency of these meetings can offer participants something to look forward to, thereby breaking the monotony of waiting. An effective guideline for running these groups includes setting an agenda that allows everyone to speak, sharing resources like books or articles on coping strategies, and organizing occasional fun activities to lighten the mood. Remember, the ultimate goal is to create a supportive environment that fosters emotional resilience.

Engaging in Church CommunityAnother invaluable resource for emotional support is the local church community. Churches are not just places of worship but are also hubs for fellowship and mutual care. Participating in church activities can offer spiritual sustenance and practical support, helping to stabilize emotions during uncertain times.

Churches often organize events, workshops, and prayer groups which can serve as fantastic opportunities to connect with others facing similar challenges. In addition to emotional support, churches frequently offer practical assistance through charitable programs, counseling services, and volunteer opportunities. Engaging in these activities not only provides a sense of purpose but also shifts focus away from personal struggles, making the waiting period more bearable.

Sharing Stories of WaitingThere is incredible power in storytelling. By sharing personal experiences of waiting, individuals can forge deeper connections and foster a sense of solidarity. When people openly discuss their struggles, they not only lighten their own emotional load but also help others realize they are not alone in their ordeal.

In support groups or church communities, encouraging members to share their stories can break the ice and create stronger bonds. Personal narratives of waiting can offer valuable lessons, new perspectives, and unique coping strategies. Moreover, hearing someone else's story can ignite hope and motivate others to persist through their own waiting periods.

Creating a space where storytelling is encouraged involves fostering an environment of trust and confidentiality. Participants should feel safe to express their thoughts and emotions without fear of judgment.

Over time, these shared stories can become sources of inspiration and resilience for the entire community.

Offering and Requesting HelpBuilding a culture of mutual aid is another crucial aspect of navigating emotional challenges. Encouraging both offering and requesting help within a community empowers individuals and promotes collective well-being.

When people actively help each other, it creates a cycle of generosity and support that benefits everyone involved. Whether it's offering a listening ear, assisting with daily tasks, or simply being present, acts of kindness can significantly alleviate emotional stress. Equally important is learning to ask for help when needed. Many people hesitate to seek assistance due to feelings of pride or fear of burdening others, but requesting help is a sign of strength, not weakness.

Communities thrive when they adopt a give-and-take approach. Organizing initiatives like a buddy system, where pairs check in on each other regularly, can ensure no one feels neglected. Setting up a community message board or an online group chat for people to post their needs and offers of help can streamline the process and make support more accessible.

Conclusion

Final Thoughts

So there you have it, dear reader, a smorgasbord of strategies to make the unbearable bearable. Whether you're grounding yourself in the present with mindfulness, sending up breath prayers like spiritual SOS flares, or flexing your muscles in the name of both fitness and sanity, you've got a toolkit ready for action. Waiting might never be fun, but with these tips, at least it's less likely to drive you to chocolate-fueled madness.

Remember, waiting doesn't have to be a time of aimless thumb-twiddling. Turn those idle moments into opportunities for growth and peace. Next time you're staring down the barrel of an endless wait, whip out these techniques and show anxiety who's boss. After all, isn't it better to face life's delays with calm assurance than to let them steal your joy? So breathe deep, stay present, and maybe even get a little creative—because you've got this waiting game all figured out.

Chapter Five

Waiting Together: The Power of Community

Waiting can be a real exercise in patience, but waiting together as a community brings a whole other dimension to the experience. When you're stuck in that awkward space between longing and fulfillment, having companions by your side can turn those anxious moments into opportunities for connection and growth. Whether it's sharing personal stories, joining group prayers, or compiling collective wisdom in waiting journals, being part of a supportive community can make waiting periods less isolating and even enriching.

In this chapter, we'll explore how communal support plays a pivotal role during these waiting times. You'll discover the power of vulnerability and how it opens doors for deeper relationships. We'll look at inspiring personal testimonies, practical activities like journaling initiatives, and the impact of group prayers on fostering a sense of unity. Through shared experiences within a faith community, we'll see how individual journeys can be enriched, making the wait a little more bearable—and maybe even a bit more joyful!

Sharing Experiences to Foster Connection

Sharing personal stories during times of waiting can act as a powerful tool for creating deep connections within the community. When individuals openly share their struggles, it invites empathy and understanding from others. This openness fosters an environment where people feel safe expressing their feelings, knowing they will not be judged but rather supported. Empathy is a critical element in these scenarios—it builds bridges between individuals, making them feel less isolated while affirming that their experiences and emotions are valid.

Vulnerability, although often seen as a weakness, is one of the strongest pillars in cultivating deeper relationships. When someone dares to be vulnerable, it encourages others to do the same, breaking down barriers of isolation. Imagine a group meeting where people talk about their waiting periods—whether it's for a medical diagnosis, a job offer, or a life change. These moments of truth-telling promote mutual encouragement. When you see that others have the courage to share, it emboldens you to open up as well. This relational depth then becomes the bedrock upon which a supportive community thrives.

Personal testimonies have an incredible ability to inspire and uplift others who might be experiencing similar challenges. Take, for instance, a person waiting for a breakthrough in their spiritual life or a resolution to a prolonged illness. When they hear a testimony about God's presence in such situations, it can light a spark of hope within them. The stories act as reminders that they are not alone in their wait, reinforcing the idea that there is a divine purpose even in the most trying times. These stories can come from anywhere—past sermons, published books, or even a casual conversation during a community gathering. The point is, shared narratives make the waiting period more bearable by illustrating that patience and faith can lead to profound personal growth.

One effective method to keep these testimonies alive is through a waiting journal initiative. In this initiative, community members document their experiences, thoughts, and emotions as they go through their waiting periods. These journals can serve multiple purposes. Firstly, they provide an outlet for individuals to express themselves, offering a sense of relief and clarity. Secondly, when shared, these journals become a collective repository of wisdom, providing insights and lessons learned that can benefit everyone in the community. Thirdly, they foster accountability and hope. Knowing that your journey will be read by others can motivate you to stay positive and faithful, drawing strength from the collective narrative.

Creating a waiting journal can seem like a simple task, but its impact can be profound. It allows for continuous reflection and documentation, helping individuals track their emotional and spiritual growth. Moreover, sharing entries from these journals during community meetings or on social media can encourage others to start their own. Anyone can begin by jotting down daily thoughts or significant events, gradually building a comprehensive narrative. Over time, these journals can transform into valuable resources that highlight the resilience and faith of the community.

Incorporating group prayer sessions can also significantly enhance the sense of community. When people pray together, especially in a

structured setting that focuses on specific waiting periods, it creates
a unique bond. A prayer session could start with reading excerpts
from the waiting journals, followed by open discussions and collective
prayers. This not only brings people closer but also strengthens their
spiritual connection. Group prayers serve as a powerful reminder that
no one waits alone—their struggles and hopes are shared and lifted by
the entire community.

The power of communal support during waiting periods cannot be
overstated. Each shared story acts like a thread, weaving individuals
together into a tapestry of shared experience and mutual encouragement. As people disclose their vulnerabilities, engage in heartfelt
conversations, and participate in collective activities like journaling
and group prayers, the community grows stronger and more resilient.
This interconnectedness transforms the daunting prospect of waiting
into an opportunity for deep personal and communal growth.

Building a Supportive Faith Community

Cultivating a nurturing and supportive faith community is like planting seeds in fertile soil - it requires intention, effort, and care. One effective approach to building such a community is through the forma-
tion of small groups centered around waiting themes. These groups
can become powerful spaces for mutual encouragement, relation-
ship-building, and sharing experiences.

Imagine a group of individuals meeting weekly to discuss their personal journeys of waiting – whether it's waiting for healing, for a
job opportunity, or for a loved one to come to faith. In these spaces,
members can freely share their struggles, triumphs, and lessons learned
along the way. By focusing on common themes, these groups create

an environment where everyone feels understood and supported. The shared experience of waiting helps forge strong bonds among participants, fostering a sense of belonging and collective strength.

In addition to forming small groups, involvement in community service or church activities plays a significant role in strengthening communal ties. When people engage in acts of service together, they not only support a common cause but also develop deeper relationships with each other. Volunteering at food banks, organizing charity events, or participating in mission trips are just a few examples of how serving others can bring a community closer. These activities emphasize shared purpose and create a sense of fulfillment, reminding everyone that they are part of something greater than themselves.

Mentorship opportunities within the faith community are equally vital. Seasoned believers, having walked the path of faith longer, possess invaluable wisdom and insights that can guide those currently navigating periods of waiting. Mentors can provide advice, offer prayers, and share stories of how they have experienced God's faithfulness during their own times of waiting. This relationship nurtures patience and trust in God, reinforcing the idea that waiting is not a passive state but an active period of growth and dependence on divine timing. Moreover, mentorship can occur in various forms, from face-to-face meetings to virtual interactions, ensuring that guidance and support are accessible to all.

Utilizing social media and online platforms effectively broadens the support network for a faith community. Technology allows for instant communication, facilitating prayer requests, sharing of inspirational content, and virtual meet-ups. For instance, a church could create a dedicated Facebook group where members can post updates, share devotionals, and offer encouragement to one another. This digital space enables connection beyond geographical boundaries, making it possible for people to stay engaged and supported even when they cannot meet in person. According to Leake (2024), technology has played a pivotal role in missions and ministry, allowing for deep and meaningful connections to be built globally.

One practical guideline for establishing support groups is to ensure they are inclusive and welcoming. Encourage members to participate actively, share their thoughts, and listen empathetically to others. Regularly scheduled meetings and structured discussions can help maintain focus and consistency. Additionally, rotating leadership roles within the group can give everyone a sense of ownership and responsibility.

When engaging in communal activities, it's beneficial to align efforts with the interests and skills of the community members. Identify causes that resonate with the group's values and encourage collective participation. Providing variety in the activities can maintain enthusiasm and commitment over time.

For mentorship opportunities, it's helpful to pair mentors and mentees thoughtfully, considering factors such as personality compatibility and shared life experiences. Regular check-ins and open communication are key to maintaining a productive mentorship relationship. Offering training sessions for potential mentors can equip them with the necessary skills to provide effective support.

When leveraging social media and online platforms, establish clear guidelines for respectful and uplifting communication. Moderators can help manage the content and ensure the virtual space remains safe and encouraging for all members. Also, consider utilizing various forms of digital content like videos, podcasts, and blog posts to keep the community engaged and inspired.

Biblical Examples of Collective Waiting

The Israelites in the wilderness represent a profound example of communal waiting and reliance on God's provision. When they left Egypt, they found themselves wandering through barren lands, often questioning their purpose and future. Yet, it was in these moments of uncertainty that their faith as a community was tested and ultimately strengthened. They relied on God's daily provision of manna from heaven, showing that waiting can serve divine purposes beyond immediate understanding. The collective experience of depending on God for their physical sustenance taught them a deeper spiritual lesson about trust and patience. Their shared struggles and triumphs bound them together, making their journey not just a physical relocation but a spiritual transformation as well.

Similarly, the early Christians' collective prayer after Christ's ascension provides another powerful symbol of unified waiting. Acts 1:14 describes how they "all joined together constantly in prayer," seeking guidance and strength from the Holy Spirit. This communal act of prayer wasn't just an expression of their dependence on God but also a means to discern His will collectively. The early church set an example of how unified prayer can become a cornerstone for decision-making and reassurance during uncertain times. It's fascinating to see how these early Christians, despite facing persecution and immense challenges, drew strength from each other through prayer. Their collective faith became a beacon of hope and direction, reinforcing the idea that waiting together with a common purpose can lead to profound spiritual insights and actions.

Moses and Aaron's collaborative leadership during the Exodus illustrates the significance of supportive relationships in a period of prolonged waiting. Leading a multitude of people through the desert required enormous patience, wisdom, and mutual support. Moses, overwhelmed by the burden of leadership, leaned on Aaron and others to share responsibilities, creating a system of delegated authority. This collaboration allowed for sustained and effective leadership, demonstrating that collective growth and shared burdens are crucial during challenging times. Leaders like Moses and Aaron relied on each other's strengths, teaching us that supportive relationships foster resilience and long-term success, especially when navigating through difficult phases.

Esther's story exemplifies the necessity of strategic, communal engagement while awaiting divine intervention. Faced with the annihilation of her people, Esther didn't act alone. She called for a fast among the Jewish community, asking everyone to abstain from food and drink while she did the same. This collective act of fasting served as both a plea for divine favor and a means to unite the community in a shared purpose. Esther's preparation and the community's solidarity highlight the power of combined efforts and strategic planning when waiting for a critical resolution. It underscores the importance of rallying communal support and engaging in concerted actions, reinforcing that communal faith can move mountains even in the direst situations.

In all these biblical examples, we see the recurring theme of communal waiting serving larger divine purposes. Whether it's the Israelites learning to trust God's provision, early Christians discovering the power of unified prayer, or figures like Moses, Aaron, and Esther showcasing the importance of collaboration and strategic engagement, the Bible is rich with stories that highlight the power of waiting within a community context. These narratives teach us that waiting isn't just a passive state but an active period where faith, unity, and collective action play pivotal roles in achieving greater goals.

The experiences of these biblical communities remind us that individual journeys often gain depth and meaning when shared with others. Through collective faith, believers find strength, guidance, and support that might be elusive when faced with challenges alone. These examples urge modern faith communities to embrace the principles of waiting together, leaning on each other's strengths, praying collectively, and engaging in unified actions to navigate through periods of uncertainty.

Insights and Implications

As we draw to the end of our discussion on communal support, it's clear that sharing personal stories during times of waiting isn't just a nice-to-have; it's a lifeline. We've seen that being open about our struggles invites empathy and builds strong connections, making us all feel a little less alone in our journeys. Everyone's tales of vulnerability turn into a collective treasure trove of wisdom and encouragement. Whether we're pondering our next career move or waiting for some divine intervention, these shared experiences make the wait more bearable and even enriching.

Adding a dash of humor and shared journal entries can transform the serious business of waiting into something that feels like a community project. Group prayers, storytelling sessions, and small group meet-ups become the glue that binds us together. The journey turns from a solitary trek through the wilderness into an engaging team expedition. So, as you go forth, remember: your story matters. Share it, listen to others, laugh a little, and find strength in the communal waiting game. Who knew waiting could be such a fun and spiritually enriching activity?

Chapter Six

Active Engagement During Waiting

Transforming the experience of waiting from a passive state into active engagement can make all the difference. Instead of grumbling about wasted time or staring blankly at the clock, imagine diving headfirst into activities that spark joy and ignite your creativity! Whether it's unleashing your inner artist with some paintbrushes, crafting a gourmet meal out of random pantry finds, or even pottering about in the garden, these moments become golden opportunities. Engaging in purposeful hobbies doesn't just keep boredom at bay; it lets you tap into reservoirs of passion, making time fly and enriching your life in unexpected ways. Picture how fulfilling it feels to see a painting come to life on a canvas, or to taste a dish that's worthy of a five-star rating—all products of time well-spent.

In this chapter, we'll explore heaps of fantastic strategies to transform idle waiting periods into proactive, soul-nourishing experiences.

You'll discover how setting short-term goals can offer a sense of direction and achievement, turning otherwise interminable waits into a sequence of rewarding milestones. We'll also dive into the power of human connection and how engaging with others, whether through old friendships or new community ties, can provide both solace and fresh perspectives. Additionally, if you've ever considered picking up a new skill or deepening your spiritual knowledge, now's the time! From learning an instrument to delving deeper into biblical texts, the avenues are endless. So, buckle up as we turn the mundane act of waiting into a vibrant journey filled with faith, purpose, and plenty of laughter along the way.

Engaging in Purposeful Activities While Waiting

Staying proactive during periods of waiting can be a game-changer. Instead of twiddling your thumbs, why not dive into activities that ignite your passion and creativity? Purposeful hobbies serve as a fantastic way to keep your spirit engaged while you wait. Think about it: Have you ever noticed how time flies when you're engrossed in something you love? Whether it's painting, writing, gardening, or even cooking, these hobbies can be incredibly fulfilling.

Imagine picking up a brush and letting your imagination run wild on a canvas. Not only does this spark creativity, but it also provides a sense of accomplishment. Moreover, such hobbies can end up being deeply enriching for your spiritual life. By dedicating time to activities that make your heart sing, you create a reservoir of joy and satisfaction. These positive emotions can, in turn, foster resilience, making the waiting period much more bearable.

Now, let's talk about setting short-term goals. It might sound like a corporate strategy, but establishing achievable milestones can work wonders even in everyday life. If you've ever faced an uncertain time, you know how easy it is to feel adrift. Setting short-term goals can provide a much-needed anchor. Why wait for a grand goal when you can start with smaller ones?

Picture this: You're waiting for a significant life change, like a job offer or an important decision. Meanwhile, set a goal to read a chapter of a book every day, master a new recipe, or even learn a few new words in a foreign language each week. These small achievements build momentum. Each time you check something off your list, you get a small dose of accomplishment. It's like giving yourself a high-five for keeping it together despite the uncertainty around you.

Another aspect of staying proactive during times of waiting involves building connections. Humans are social creatures by nature, and strengthening relationships can offer immense support and encouragement. This is where the power of community comes into play. Engaging with others can be a source of both distraction and inspiration.

Ever had a conversation that left you feeling lighter and more hopeful? That's the magic of human connection. Reach out to friends and family, or even make new acquaintances through interest groups or social media. Sharing experiences and offering mutual support can transform the way you perceive waiting. When you're surrounded by people who care, waiting doesn't seem as daunting. Plus, these connections often bring fresh perspectives and ideas, helping you navigate through your period of waiting with renewed energy.

Of course, let's not forget about learning new skills or deepening bib-lical knowledge. The waiting period can be seen as a gift of time—an opportunity to invest in yourself. Why not use this time to take up an online course, attend a workshop, or read books that expand your horizons? Learning something new can be incredibly invigorating.

Consider learning a new instrument, immersing yourself in a subject you've always been curious about, or studying the Bible in greater depth. Each of these activities not only fills the waiting time but also enriches your mind and soul. When you come out on the other side, you do so not just as someone who's waited, but as someone who's grown.

Let's delve deeper into how purposeful hobbies can truly ignite pas-sion and creativity. For instance, if you've always had an interest in photography, now is the perfect time to explore it further. With a camera or even just your smartphone, you can capture moments from your daily life. Over time, you may find yourself looking at things differently, noticing details you previously overlooked. This new per-spective can spill over into other aspects of your life, making you more mindful and appreciative of the world around you.

Similarly, engaging in crafts like knitting or woodworking can be in-credibly therapeutic. The act of creating something with your hands brings a sense of fulfillment and helps in focusing your mind. It's like meditative therapy where you lose track of time and immerse yourself fully in the activity.

In terms of setting short-term goals, imagine you're waiting for res-olution on a long-term project at work. Instead of stressing over the outcome, break your time into manageable chunks with specific objectives. Perhaps you decide to complete a part of another project, update your professional skills, or simply organize your workspace. Each mini-goal achieved boosts your confidence and keeps you moving forward.

When it comes to building connections, think of the countless opportunities out there. Join a local club or online group related to your interests. Engage in discussions, share your thoughts, and listen to others. Not only does this broaden your social circle, but it also introduces you to a variety of viewpoints. This exchange of ideas and experiences can be incredibly enriching.

Lastly, utilizing waiting time for learning can lead to surprising benefits. Let's say you're interested in learning a new language. There are numerous apps and online resources available. Dedicate a small portion of your day to practice. Over time, you'll not only acquire a new skill but also open doors to understanding different cultures.

Deepening biblical knowledge can be equally rewarding. Take some quiet time each day to read and reflect upon the scriptures. Join a Bible study group or follow online sermons. Discussing these insights with others can deepen your understanding and enhance your faith.

Spiritual Disciplines to Maintain Focus

Waiting isn't just a passive activity; it can be an opportunity for growth and deeper spiritual connection. One way to transform waiting into a spiritually enriching experience is by practicing various spiritual disciplines. These practices not only keep us centered but also help us maintain our focus on God.

Committing time for prayer is one of the most effective ways to nurture a closer connection with God during periods of waiting. Prayer is more than just a list of petitions; it's a conversation with God that allows us to pour out our hearts and listen for His guidance. Think of it as calling your best friend to catch up—it provides comfort and assurance that you're not alone. Creating a specific time each day dedicated to prayer can build continuity and depth in your relationship with God. It's like scheduling a recurring coffee date that you always look forward to.

Alongside prayer, dedicating time each day to study the Word strengthens trust in divine timing. The Bible is a treasure trove of wisdom, encouragement, and promises that can sustain us through long periods of waiting. By immersing ourselves in scripture, we are reminded of God's faithfulness throughout history, which reassures us that He remains faithful in our lives too. It's like reading a series of love letters from God, reminding us how deeply He cares and how meticulously He plans everything for our good.

Fasting is another powerful discipline that fosters deeper reliance on God and His timing. Fasting isn't merely about abstaining from food; it's about prioritizing spiritual nourishment over physical cravings. By setting aside meals or certain types of food, we make space to seek God more earnestly. Through fasting, we learn to depend on Him for strength and clarity, realizing that our true sustenance comes from Him. It's like temporarily unplugging from all distractions to tune into a frequency that brings us closer to divine revelations. Remember what Jesus said in Matthew 6:16, "When you fast..."—it's an expectation, not an option (fueledfitfocused@gmail.com, 2020).

Keeping a journal can also be immensely beneficial during times of waiting. Journaling helps capture thoughts, prayers, and lessons learned, providing a tangible record of our spiritual journey. Writing down experiences and insights can reveal patterns and progress that might otherwise go unnoticed. It's akin to keeping a travel diary during an extended trip, allowing reflection on where you've been, and giving hope and direction for where you're heading. When you revisit your journal entries, you'll see how God has answered prayers and how you've grown through the waiting period.

Now, let's break down these practices with some guidelines for maximizing their benefits:

Prayer and Meditation: Set aside a quiet place and a specific time each day for prayer. Begin with a few deep breaths to center yourself, then start talking to God as you would with a friend. Incorporate both speaking and listening into your prayer time. Sometimes, sitting in silence can be profoundly revealing as you wait for the Holy Spirit's guidance.

Reading Scripture: Choose a systematic approach to studying the Bible. This could be following a reading plan, focusing on a particular book, or even doing topical studies. Take notes, highlight passages, and consider using commentaries or study guides for deeper understanding. Reflect on how the scriptures apply to your current situation and record these reflections in your journal.

Fasting: Decide on the type of fast you will undertake, whether it's abstaining from all food, specific meals, or certain types of food. Start with a clear purpose—what are you seeking from God?—and use the time you would spend eating to pray and read scripture. Stay hydrated and remember that it's okay to adjust your fast according to your physical needs. If you're fasting with others, like a group or community, share your experiences and support each other through the process (Patterson, 2021).

Journaling Spiritual Insights: Keep your journal handy and write regularly. Start each entry by noting the date and any significant events or feelings you're experiencing. Write out your prayers, including both requests and thanksgiving. Record any scriptures that speak to you and document any dreams, visions, or impressions you receive during prayer or meditation. Over time, your journal will become a precious keepsake of your spiritual growth and God's faithfulness.

Volunteering and Service as Forms of Active Waiting

Engaging in service and volunteerism during periods of waiting is a powerful way to turn idle time into an opportunity for growth and purpose. Rather than becoming consumed by impatience or self-focus, one can find healing and fulfillment through helping others and contributing to the community. This proactive approach not only benefits those in need but also brings about personal transformation.

Finding opportunities to serve begins with identifying areas where assistance is needed. Instead of fixating on personal challenges, looking outward offers a new perspective. Volunteering in settings such as local shelters, food banks, or community centers provides a sense of purpose. The act of serving shifts focus from oneself to the greater good, fostering a sense of connection and empathy.

Joining community service projects offers structured opportunities to make a difference. These projects often require efforts from multiple volunteers, encouraging teamwork and collaboration. Whether participating in environmental cleanup initiatives, organizing charity drives, or building homes for those in need, engaging in collective efforts has a way of bringing people together. It creates a support network where individuals can share experiences, lean on each other, and achieve common goals. Through these experiences, participants often discover they have more in common with others than they initially thought.

Offering guidance to those in need transforms both the mentor and mentee. Acting as a mentor or coach to someone navigating difficult circumstances is immensely rewarding. Sharing knowledge, providing emotional support, or offering practical advice allows mentors to play a pivotal role in another's journey. The experience enriches the lives of both parties, fostering mutual respect and understanding. Mentors often find that guiding others helps clarify their own values and strengthen their resolve, leading to personal growth alongside their mentees.

Engaging in church groups and service opportunities can significantly enhance communal faith. Churches frequently offer various avenues for participation, from ministry teams and community outreach to supporting church administration and special events (10 Ways How to Recruit Volunteers for Church, 2024). By joining these groups, individuals contribute to the broader mission of the church while also nurturing their own spiritual well-being. Singing in the choir, helping with Sunday school, or assisting in organizing church activities can deepen one's faith and sense of belonging. Participating in these functions emphasizes the unity and shared purpose among congregants, reinforcing the strength of communal worship and service.

For instance, community outreach programs within churches extend beyond the walls of the sanctuary, addressing critical social issues such as homelessness or hunger (10 Ways How to Recruit Volunteers for Church, 2024). Being a part of these programs not only meets immediate needs but also builds bridges between the church and the surrounding community. The dedication shown by volunteers in these efforts exemplifies living faith in action, encouraging others to get involved and advocate for change.

Moreover, volunteering does not require grand gestures. Simple acts like visiting the elderly, tutoring students, or offering transportation to those without can make a significant impact. These small yet meaningful contributions remind us of our capacity for kindness and reinforce the value of every individual's effort.

Church leaders play a crucial role in encouraging volunteerism. Personal invitations to join serve as an effective method for recruiting dedicated volunteers (10 Ways How to Recruit Volunteers for Church, 2024). When current volunteers and church leaders reach out personally to members, it instills a sense of being valued and recognized. This personalized approach makes individuals feel more connected to the church's mission and motivates them to participate actively.

Highlighting the specific needs within the church and outlining the roles helps potential volunteers understand where they can best contribute. Clear communication regarding tasks and the goals of these roles fosters a sense of urgency and importance, driving home the message that everyone's contribution matters. Training and supporting volunteers ensure they feel confident and equipped to fulfill their responsibilities. Celebrating their achievements further reinforces their sense of accomplishment and belonging, creating a positive feedback loop of gratitude and motivation (Shutt, 2024).

Flexibility in volunteer roles is essential, especially during dynamic seasons like summer when personal schedules vary widely. Offering a range of opportunities that cater to different availability and skill sets ensures that volunteering remains accessible and enjoyable for everyone. Incorporating family-friendly volunteer options can also encourage collective participation, fostering a supportive and inclusive church environment.

Final Thoughts

As we've explored, turning the waiting game into an active and engaging experience can be incredibly rewarding. By diving into hobbies that spark joy and creativity, setting manageable short-term goals, building meaningful connections, and expanding our knowledge, we create a vibrant and fulfilling life even while in limbo. These activities not only fill the time but also enrich our minds, hearts, and souls, providing a strong foundation to stand on during uncertain times. Imagine coming out the other end of a waiting period not just as someone who waited, but as someone who grew, learned, and thrived.

So, let's take that waiting period by the horns and turn it into a time of active engagement and purposeful living. Whether you're picking up a paintbrush, reading a new book, chatting with friends, or learning a new skill, every moment spent actively is a moment well-lived. Embrace these strategies and see how they transform your perspective on waiting. Life doesn't pause because we're waiting for something; in fact, it's moving forward with every proactive step we take. So why not make those steps count and enjoy the journey as much as possible?

Chapter Seven

Hearing God's Voice

Hearing God's voice can feel a bit like trying to catch a whisper in a windstorm. There's noise, chaos, and a whole lot of distractions coming at you from every direction. But amid all the daily hustle and bustle, finding that quiet moment to truly listen can open up new dimensions of spiritual clarity. Imagine for a moment being in a bustling marketplace with vendors shouting, kids laughing, and music blaring. Now, try to hear the gentle rustling of leaves nearby—challenging, right? That's what our minds go through on a daily basis, making it tough to pick out God's subtle nudges amid the cacophony of life.

In this chapter, we'll dive headfirst into practices that can help sharpen our spiritual listening skills. You'll learn about carving out moments of silence amidst your busy schedule, transforming prayer from a one-sided monologue to an enriching conversation, and harnessing the power of scripture meditation as a guiding light during waiting periods. Additionally, we'll explore how fasting can heighten your awareness of God's presence, making space for divine whispers in the static of everyday life. So, buckle up and get ready to tune into a frequency that might just change how you navigate those inevitable waiting periods.

Practices for Sharpening Spiritual Listening

In the hustle and bustle of daily life, carving out moments of silence can often seem like an enormous challenge. Yet, it's precisely in these quiet moments that our minds can be calmed, making room to hear God's direction more clearly. Picture this: you're in a crowded room with multiple conversations happening simultaneously. Trying to focus on one voice can be nearly impossible amidst the noise. Our minds operate similarly. When we constantly have stimuli bombarding us, it becomes challenging to discern God's gentle whispers.

To cultivate silence, find a space where you can be alone and free from distractions. This could be a quiet corner of your home, a bench in a serene park, or even your car parked somewhere peaceful. Once there, take a few deep breaths, let go of the clamoring thoughts, and just sit in stillness. Embrace the quiet—it's God's invitation to connect with you. Allow your mind to settle, and just listen. Silence isn't about absence; it's about presence—God's presence.

Moving from silence to prayer, it's essential to evolve into viewing prayer not as a monologue but a dynamic dialogue. Too often, we may treat prayer like sending a voicemail to God, listing our worries, wants, and gratitude without pausing for a response. Instead, envision prayer as a conversation over coffee with a trusted friend. You speak, but you also listen intently, expecting a reply. When you pray, express your thoughts and feelings honestly, then wait in expectation. Ask open-ended questions like "What do you want to show me today, Lord?" or "How should I approach this situation?"

Listening prayer is a powerful tool here. Start by presenting your request to God. Then, sit in quiet anticipation, believing that He will speak to you. It's in the still, small moments that His guidance often comes through most clearly. According to Jim Harrison, "Listening prayer centers around a clear request for God's guidance...we wait on God in a time of silence, giving the Lord opportunity to speak to us" (Harrison, 2019). This practice requires patience and trust, but with consistency, you'll find yourself tuning into His voice more naturally.

Scripture meditation adds another layer of illumination during waiting periods. The Bible is filled with verses that resonate differently at various points in our lives, providing clarity and encouragement when needed most. Imagine flipping through the pages and feeling a verse jump out at you, much like finding a note left by a dear friend. These verses can become anchors in times of uncertainty. For instance, Joshua 1:9 reminds us, "Do not be afraid; do not be discouraged, for the Lord your God will be with you wherever you go." Holding onto such promises helps navigate the murky waters of waiting.

Deliberately choose scriptures that speak to your current circumstances. Write them down, memorize them, and revisit them often. Keep a journal to reflect on how these verses speak to you over time. This active engagement with God's Word allows Him to communicate with you directly, reinforcing His presence and guidance.

Fasting is another meaningful practice to heighten awareness of God's presence. Often misunderstood as merely abstaining from food, fasting is about creating space to focus on God. Think of it as turning down the volume of life's demands so you can hear the divine insights you've been missing. Fasting might involve giving up meals, social media, or other activities that consume your attention and instead dedicating that time to seeking God.

Engaging in a fast shows your earnest desire to connect more deeply with Him. As Phylicia Masonheimer notes, "Fasting is such an important part of prayer because it gives a sense of urgency to our prayers, showing that we are urgently seeking God's face" (Deyoung, 2024). During a fast, your physical hunger serves as a reminder of your spiritual hunger—prompting you to turn to God for sustenance and clarity.

Practically, start with a short fast if you're new to the practice. Maybe skip one meal and spend that time in prayer and reflection instead. Gradually, as you grow more accustomed to fasting, extend it to longer periods. Always ensure that your health permits the kind of fasting you choose. Remember, the goal is not deprivation but devotion—drawing nearer to God by setting aside ordinary routines.

Incorporating these practices—silence, conversational prayer, scripture meditation, and fasting—creates a robust framework for hearing and understanding God's voice. Each practice complements the others, fostering an environment where you can discern His guidance more clearly, especially during those trying waiting periods.

Take this journey one step at a time. Allow yourself grace as you incorporate these habits into your life. There will be days when silence feels impossible, prayer feels one-sided, scriptures seem silent, and fasting seems daunting. But persist. Each effort draws you closer to recognizing God's voice amidst the noise of everyday life.

Recognizing and Interpreting Signs

Equipping Readers to Identify and Understand God's Signs During Waiting Periods

Life has its fair share of waiting periods, whether it's waiting for a promotion, clarity in relationships, or simply understanding what comes next. But during these times, how do we recognize God's voice amid the silence? Let's dive deep into practical ways you can begin to discern His guidance.

First, look to nature. Observing natural phenomena can serve as powerful reminders of God's promises and His ever-present nature. Think about the rainbow after a storm; not just a pretty sight, but a symbol of God's covenant with Noah, a promise of faithfulness. Ever taken a walk in the park and felt an inexplicable peace watching the birds? They remind us of God's provision, as emphasized in Matthew 6:26: "Look at the birds of the air; they do not sow or reap or store away in barns, and yet your heavenly Father feeds them." In the same way, when we see flowers blooming or the sun rising, these everyday miracles can reassure us of God's continuous presence and care.

Now, let's consider our personal circumstances. Sometimes, life's twists and turns can seem random, but there is often hidden meaning when viewed through the lens of prayer. For example, losing a job might feel like a setback initially, but it could be God's way of steering you towards a path better aligned with your divine purpose. Therefore, analyzing life's events through dedicated prayer can open our eyes to God's provision and direction. It's like having a spiritual magnifying glass that helps you see beyond the surface.

Moving on to community interaction, engaging in discussions with fellow believers can significantly enhance our understanding of the signs recognized. Proverbs 27:17 says, "As iron sharpens iron, so one person sharpens another." Conversations with friends, attending Bible study groups, or even casual dialogues over coffee can provide fresh perspectives and insights that you may not have considered. Your peers can act as sounding boards, helping to interpret confusing signs and affirm God's voice in your life. Remember, it's incredibly comforting and enriching to have a team of spiritual detectives working alongside you.

Another crucial aspect is trusting your gut feelings. Often, we hear people say, "I felt it in my bones," or "something didn't feel right." These are not just idle chatter; in many cases, these gut instincts are promptings from the Holy Spirit guiding us in a particular direction. When facing tough decisions during times of waiting, pay attention to these inner nudges. If a certain path brings you peace, even though it may seem challenging, it might be God's way of telling you that you're on the right track. Conversely, if a choice leaves you restless and uneasy, take it as a cue to rethink. Philippians 4:7 speaks of "the peace of God, which transcends all understanding," acting as a sentinel for your heart and mind, especially when making critical choices.

To bring this all together, let's revisit these points with some actionable guidelines:

1. **Nature and Creation:** Take time each day to observe your surroundings. Whether it's a morning jog or a brief pause during your lunch break, allow yourself to marvel at the simple wonders around you. Use these moments as reminders of God's promises and his omnipresence.

2. **Circumstantial Indicators:** Keep a prayer journal to record life's significant events and your prayers concerning them. Over time, review these entries to identify patterns and answers that reveal God's hand at work. This practice not only enhances your ability to recognize divine intervention but also strengthens your relationship with God through consistent communication.

3. **Community Affirmation:** Make it a habit to discuss your spiritual journey with trusted individuals in your faith community. Organize regular meet-ups or join existing small groups where you can share experiences and seek counsel. The goal is to foster a support network eager to help you decode God's messages.

4. **Inner Peace as Confirmation:** Practice mindfulness to become more attuned to your inner feelings. When faced with decisions, pause and pray for discernment. Trust the sense of peace or unrest that follows as a gauge to evaluate your choices.

Distinguishing Between God's Voice and Personal Desires

Understanding the difference between divine guidance and our own personal urges during periods of waiting can be as confusing as trying to navigate through a foggy forest. However, with some introspection and a few helpful guidelines, we can begin to see the light and follow a clearer path.

Firstly, reflecting on our underlying motives is crucial. When we desire something deeply, it's easy to convince ourselves that it's God's will rather than our own aspirations whispering sweet nothings in our ears. Take a moment to ask yourself: "Why do I want this? Is it for my glory or for God's?" This self-inquiry, though simple, can often reveal whether the compass of your heart is set to divine north or veering off into wishful thinking territory.

Moreover, God's voice always harmonizes with the principles outlined in the Bible, which serve as our foundational guide. When discerning if a nudge or inclination is from God, align it against biblical teachings. If what you feel led to do runs contrary to Scripture, it's a clear indicator that you might be chasing after a mirage rather than following divine direction. To quote one ancient sage (whose name surely escapes me), "God isn't going to tell you something that goes against His Word. It's like expecting a vegan to recommend a steakhouse."

Now, let's talk about the fruits of your actions. Actions stemming from God will produce positive fruit, such as love, joy, and peace. Picture this: You decide to act on what you believe is a divine prompt and start a community garden. Soon, your neighborhood blossoms—not just with tomatoes and sunflowers, but with renewed camaraderie and joy. The peace of knowing you're walking in God's will often surpasses understanding. On the other hand, if your "divine" idea leads only to stress, confusion, and discord, it may be time to reconsider its source.

During uncertain times, seeking counsel within your faith community can be incredibly beneficial. Accountability plays a critical role here. Sharing your desires and perceived guidance with trusted members of your faith community allows for external confirmation. Remember, even Sherlock Holmes had Watson! Your fellow believers can provide valuable insights, helping separate divine nudges from misguided impulses. They might gently remind you of past moments when you've misinterpreted your own desires as God's will—like that time you were convinced it was divine intervention guiding you to buy that impractical but oh-so-shiny sports car.

When you share your thoughts with others, you also invite them to pray alongside you, creating an environment where collective wisdom and discernment flourish. This doesn't mean passing the responsibility onto someone else, but rather, it's about embracing the wisdom of Proverbs 11:14, which says, "Where there is no guidance, a people falls, but in an abundance of counselors there is safety."

To wrap it all up, distinguishing between divine guidance and personal urges involves deep reflection, alignment with Scripture, evaluating the fruits of your actions, and seeking accountability from your faith community. It's a bit like making soup: you need the right ingredients (motives), a good recipe (Scripture), taste tests (evaluating the fruits), and sometimes, a taste-testing panel (faith community) to get it right.

Reflecting on your underlying motives can sometimes feel like trying to pull weeds from a dense garden. Personal aspirations can easily masquerade as divine nudges, especially when they align neatly with our deepest desires. For instance, wanting a career change might genuinely come from a place of restlessness and lack of fulfillment. But take a step back: Is it because God's guiding you towards something better, or are you just yearning for a change that benefits you personally? Asking questions about the origins of our intentions can help us sift through our thoughts and feelings, ensuring that we're acting out of faith rather than selfish ambition.

The Bible serves as an unwavering touchstone when seeking to understand God's voice. Consider it a cheat sheet provided by the Ultimate Creator. Anything we believe to be divinely inspired should echo the themes and principles found in Scripture. If you feel led to embark on an action that promotes revenge, for instance—even if it feels justified—it's wise to remember that vengeance belongs to the Lord. Finding harmony between your feelings and biblical principles ensures you're on the right track. Just like how the melody line of a song must work with the chords to create harmony, so too must your inner convictions align with the eternal truths found in the Bible.

Let's delve deeper into the concept of positive fruit. Think of the Fruits of the Spirit—love, joy, peace, patience, kindness, goodness, faithfulness, gentleness, and self-control—as markers significantly indicating divine guidance. Have you ever noticed how some decisions bring about a sense of lightness, fulfillment, and serenity? That's your spiritual fruit growing! Conversely, when actions result in turmoil, bitterness, or anxiety, it's likely a sign you're steering away from God's plan. Reflect on Galatians 5:22-23, and remember that God's direction inherently cultivates these fruits within us. They are a divine confirmation, an internal "thumbs up" from the Holy Spirit.

Lastly, fostering accountability through sharing is invaluable. In involving your faith community, you not only gain different perspectives but also open yourself to correction and encouragement. Think of it as having a team of spotters while you lift weights at the gym—they're there to ensure you don't strain yourself unnecessarily and to applaud your efforts when you succeed. When discussing your desires with them, their feedback can be precious. They might point out blind spots or affirm your convictions. Recalling James 5:16, 'Therefore confess your sins to each other and pray for each other so that you may be healed', highlights the importance of such communal interactions in bolstering our spiritual journey.

Final Insights

As we wrap up our time together in this chapter, let's take a moment to chuckle at the everyday chaos that often drowns out divine whispers. Between juggling work, relationships, and finding time just to breathe, it's no wonder tuning into God's guidance feels like trying to catch a radio signal in the middle of a storm! But hey, remember those quiet moments we carved out? Whether it's sitting on a park bench or hiding in the bathroom from your kids for five minutes of peace, these are golden opportunities for fostering genuine connection with God. Silence, conversational prayer, scripture meditation, and even fasting—each practice can transform those waiting periods into rich, spiritual adventures.

Speaking of spiritual adventures, let's embrace the beauty of uncertainty. Sure, the path isn't always clear, and there might be more questions than answers at times. But each step, even the wobbly ones, gets you closer to recognizing God's voice amid life's noisy orchestra. So take these practices to heart, laugh off the awkward silences, and trust that every effort brings you nearer to experiencing His presence more vividly during those waiting periods. Keep going, keep listening, and most importantly, keep laughing along the way!

Chapter Eight

Personal Reflection and Growth

E ngaging in personal reflection is like holding up a magnifying glass to your life, highlighting areas ripe for growth that you might otherwise overlook. When we find ourselves stuck in the limbo of waiting—whether it's for a job offer, test results, or even the slow rise of homemade bread—the opportunity for self-exploration knocks on our door. Instead of letting stress and uncertainty cloud our minds, this chapter nudges us to turn inward and see these intervals as valuable pauses brimming with potential for transformation.

In this chapter, you'll discover how journaling can be an effective tool to navigate through these periods of anticipation. We'll dive into practical reflective practices, offering prompts that guide your introspection and help you clear the mental clutter. You'll also learn creative ways to incorporate art into your journaling, adding depth to your reflections. By establishing a consistent habit, identifying recurring emotional themes, and acknowledging small victories along the way, you'll uncover deeper insights about yourself. So grab that journal, ready your pen, and prepare to transform waiting from a source of frustration into a path for profound personal growth.

Journaling and Reflective Practices

Journaling is a fantastic tool for self-reflection, especially during periods of waiting when our minds can wander into the realms of stress and uncertainty. It's like having a conversation with yourself without the awkward pauses or interruptions. By putting pen to paper, you create a safe space to articulate your thoughts and feelings, giving you clarity and often surprising insights about your experiences.

Imagine this: you're stuck in a waiting game, whether it's for a job offer, a health result, or even just waiting for your sourdough bread to rise. Instead of letting anxiety take the wheel, grab a journal. This simple act of writing things down helps you empty the mental clutter that builds up. It's a bit like spring cleaning your brain, making room for more positive and constructive thoughts.

Now, if staring at a blank page gives you flashbacks to your high school exams, worry not. Utilizing prompts can guide you to explore specific aspects of your waiting experience. Prompts like "What am I waiting for and why does it matter to me?" or "What emotions am I feeling right now and what do they tell me about my needs?" can serve as gentle nudges to get the introspection ball rolling. Think of them as little breadcrumbs leading you through the dense forest of your mind.

Combining art with journaling can add another layer of personal expression. Doodling, sketching, or even incorporating photos can transform your journal into a vibrant collage of thoughts and feelings. This visual element isn't just decorative; it's therapeutic. Drawing can sometimes express what words cannot capture. You might find that a simple sketch of a blooming flower on one page and a stormy cloud on another perfectly encapsulates the highs and lows of your waiting period.

But let's face it: life gets busy, and the thought of adding yet another task to your daily routine can feel daunting. That's where establishing a regular journaling habit comes in handy. Setting aside specific times for journaling, like every evening before bed or during your morning coffee ritual, makes it a manageable part of your day. This consistency not only cultivates a healthy habit but also reinforces the practice of reflection. Over time, you'll start noticing patterns and recurring themes in your entries, offering deeper insights into your emotional landscape.

Consider the story of Amanda, a marketing executive who found herself in a spiral of stress while awaiting news on a big project. She decided to start journaling every night for ten minutes. At first, her entries were a jumble of frustrations and anxieties. But as the days passed, she began using prompts to dig deeper. One night she sketched a winding road with several obstacles. This visual representation made her realize that much like navigating a tricky path, her waiting period was full of challenges she could overcome. This epiphany gave her a newfound resilience.

Research backs up these benefits too. Journaling activates multiple areas of the brain involved in processing emotions and thoughts, helping to alleviate strong feelings like irritation and anger (Tabac, 2021).

Simply put, it engages your senses and keeps you grounded in the present moment, ultimately aiding in emotional regulation.

So, next time you find yourself twiddling your thumbs, reach for your journal instead. Use those precious moments of waiting to dive deep into your inner world. Write, doodle, reflect—and watch how this practice transforms your waiting experience from a period of uncertainty into an opportunity for profound personal growth.

To give you some practical steps, here's how you can start:

Choose a journal that excites you.

Pick a consistent time each day to write.

Begin with simple prompts to guide your reflection.

Don't worry about grammar or structure; this is your private space.

Incorporate visuals whenever you feel inspired.

Remember, there are no rules when it comes to journaling. The goal is to create a space where your thoughts and feelings can flow freely. Whether it's a sentence, a paragraph, or a doodle, every entry counts. Over time, you'll build a rich tapestry of insights, helping you navigate not just your waiting periods but all of life's twists and turns with greater ease and understanding.

Assessing Past Experiences for Growth Opportunities

Reflecting on Past Waits: Growing Through Waiting Periods

Have you ever found yourself waiting for something and felt like time was dragging on forever? Maybe it was waiting for a job offer, a medical result, or even just the next season of your favorite TV show. It's easy to think of these periods as wasted time, but what if they're actually opportunities for growth? This section will help you explore that idea by reflecting on past waiting experiences.

First off, consider how reflecting on previous waiting periods can reveal God's faithfulness in your life. Remember the story of Joseph from the Bible? He spent years in prison after being wrongfully accused, yet he remained faithful and eventually rose to a position of great power. When you look back at times you've had to wait, you might see that things eventually worked out in ways you never expected. Perhaps a delayed job offer led you to an even better opportunity, or maybe waiting for a relationship to develop taught you patience and understanding.

To delve into this, try keeping a "waiting journal." Write down past situations where you had to wait and note the outcomes. Did they turn out better than expected? Were there moments when you felt supported or guided, even if you couldn't see the full picture at the time? By documenting these experiences, you'll start to see patterns of faithfulness and support that can be incredibly encouraging.

Next, let's talk about identifying recurring themes during these waiting periods. Each time you've had to wait, you likely responded in unique ways. Were you anxious, hopeful, frustrated, or calm? Recognizing these emotional and behavioral responses can give you valuable insights into your character and coping mechanisms. For example, if you notice that you tend to get anxious during long waits, you might decide to focus on mindfulness techniques to manage anxiety in the future.

A practical exercise for this is to create a "theme map." On a piece of paper, list different waiting experiences and jot down the emotions and thoughts you had during each one. Look for commonalities. Did certain situations trigger particular feelings more than others? Understanding these trends can help you prepare better for future waiting periods, making them less stressful and more productive.

Acknowledging progress is another crucial aspect of personal growth during waiting times. Often, we're so focused on the outcome that we overlook the small victories along the way. Every step forward, no matter how tiny, is a cause for celebration. Did you learn a new skill while waiting for a job opportunity? Did you strengthen a friendship while waiting for a relationship to blossom? These are all signs of progress worth acknowledging.

One way to do this is by setting up a "progress wall" at home. Use sticky notes to write down each small victory or lesson learned during your waiting periods and stick them on the wall. Over time, you'll have a visual representation of your growth, which can reinforce your sense of purpose and achievement even when the waiting seems endless.

Now, let's address setbacks. Nobody enjoys setbacks; they can feel like the universe is conspiring against you. However, they can also serve as powerful learning experiences. Think about Mary and Joseph's journey to Bethlehem. They faced numerous obstacles, but each setback prepared them for future challenges and ultimately brought them closer together. Similarly, the breakdown before a breakthrough can often refine your faith and resilience.

To make the most of setbacks, try reframing them as opportunities for growth. When something doesn't go as planned, ask yourself, "What can I learn from this?" Maybe a failed job interview teaches you to improve your interviewing skills, or a delay in a project helps you develop better time management strategies. By viewing setbacks as lessons rather than failures, you transform them into stepping stones toward greater achievements.

For those particularly tough waiting periods, having a support system is invaluable. Share your experiences with trusted friends or family members who can provide encouragement and perspective. Sometimes, simply talking about what you're going through can ease the burden and make the wait more bearable.

Additionally, engaging in activities that align with your values and interests can make waiting periods more fulfilling. Volunteer work, hobbies, and self-improvement projects can keep you occupied and provide a sense of accomplishment. Plus, these activities often bring unexpected rewards and connections that enrich your life in ways you hadn't anticipated.

Remember the sermon lessons about taking active steps during waiting periods? Just as faith without works is dead, waiting without action can feel futile. Use this time to better yourself—whether it's updating your resume, honing your skills, or deepening your faith. Each proactive step you take not only makes the wait more manageable but also prepares you for the opportunities that lie ahead.

Setting Spiritual and Personal Development Goals

In times of waiting, it is natural to feel like you're stuck in limbo. Yet, these periods hold significant potential for personal and spiritual growth if approached intentionally. Setting spiritual and personal goals during these moments can provide purpose and direction. By aligning these goals with your faith, utilizing the SMART criteria, scheduling regular reassessments, and sharing your aspirations with trusted friends or a support group, you can transform these waiting periods into powerful opportunities for growth.

First, creating goals that align with your faith can be a guiding star. Whether it's through deeper prayer, volunteering, or other faith-based initiatives, tying your ambitions to your spiritual beliefs can offer fulfillment and direction. For instance, if your faith emphasizes compassion, setting a goal to volunteer at a local shelter could not only keep you engaged but also deepen your spirituality. This alignment ensures that your goals are more than just tasks to be completed; they become part of a larger purpose, enriching both your waiting period and your spiritual journey.

To give structure to these goals, introducing the SMART criteria can be incredibly beneficial. SMART stands for Specific, Measurable, Achievable, Relevant, and Time-bound. This framework helps clarify and organize your objectives. For example, instead of setting a vague goal like "I want to improve my prayer life," a SMART goal would be: "I will dedicate 20 minutes each morning to prayer for the next three months." This specificity makes it easier to track progress and stay focused. Moreover, celebrating small achievements along the way can boost your morale and motivate you to maintain your efforts.

Another essential aspect is establishing times for reassessment. Regular check-ins can help you stay accountable and ensure that your goals remain relevant and achievable. Set aside moments to reflect on your progress and adjust your goals as needed. Perhaps once a month, take some time to evaluate what's working and what isn't. Are you moving closer to your aims, or do adjustments need to be made? These reassessments provide an opportunity for self-reflection and adaptation, ensuring you remain on course despite any challenges or changes in circumstances.

Finally, sharing your goals with trusted friends or a support group can enhance motivation and accountability. Having someone to share your progress with can make a huge difference. Friends or community members can provide encouragement, celebrate your successes, and offer constructive feedback. For instance, if you're working towards a health-related goal, exercising with a friend or joining a fitness group can create a sense of camaraderie and accountability. This social element can transform your waiting period from solitary struggle to shared journey, enriching your relationships and providing necessary support.

Final Thoughts

Reflecting on our periods of waiting can offer profound insights and personal growth. We've explored how journaling provides a safe space for self-reflection, transforming what could be stressful moments into opportunities for clarity and understanding. By incorporating prompts and even visual elements like doodles, you can unlock deeper layers of your emotions and thoughts. Remember Amanda? Her nightly journaling sessions led her to unexpected epiphanies and newfound resilience.

Similarly, looking back at past waiting experiences can help identify patterns and recurring themes in your emotional responses. Whether it's through keeping a "waiting journal" or creating a "theme map," these practices enable you to see growth opportunities that might otherwise go unnoticed. Acknowledge the small victories, reframe setbacks as learning experiences, and lean on your support system. By doing so, you transform waiting periods from frustrating limbos into fertile grounds for personal development. So the next time you find yourself tapping your fingers impatiently, remember: with a bit of reflection and creativity, that time can become incredibly valuable.

Chapter Nine

Biblical Stories of Waiting

W aiting can be a real test of patience, and sometimes it feels like we're stuck in a perpetual game of "Are we there yet?" Such is the case with biblical stories where faith and waiting go hand-in-hand. Just when you think things couldn't get any more delayed, they do, making you wonder if there's some cosmic joke you're not in on. But fear not, these tales are packed with wisdom, humor, and lessons that make the waiting game a bit more bearable.

In this chapter, we'll delve into the lives of several biblical figures who became experts in the art of waiting. From Abraham and Sarah's 25-year wait for their promised child to the Israelites' 40-year wilderness trek that felt like a never-ending desert road trip, you'll see how these characters navigated their lengthy waits while maintaining faith. Their stories of doubt, impatience, and ultimate fulfillment will show you that even when things seem impossibly delayed, there's often a divine plan at work. So, buckle up and prepare to explore these timeless tales of faithful waiting.

The Story of Abraham and Sarah

Abraham and Sarah's story in the Bible is one of enduring patience and unwavering faith. It provides an insightful example of what it means to wait on God's timing. Despite their advanced ages, they held onto the promise of a child from God—a promise that seemed implausible given their circumstances.

God assured Abraham that he would be the father of many nations, but the immediate reality didn't match this grand promise. Abraham was 75 years old when he first received this assurance, and for the next 25 years, he and Sarah grappled with the tension between promise and fulfillment. In Genesis 17:5, God told Abraham, "No longer shall your name be called Abram, but your name shall be Abraham, for I have made you a father of many nations." This renaming was significant, yet the years rolled by without any sign of the promised child.

During this prolonged period of waiting, both Abraham and Sarah experienced moments of doubt. It's easy to understand their struggle; after all, who wouldn't feel uncertain when faced with such a delay? At one point, Sarah, tired of waiting and perhaps feeling desperate, proposed an alternative plan. She suggested that Abraham have a child with her maidservant, Hagar, thinking that maybe this was how God intended to fulfill His promise (Genesis 16). This led to the birth of Ishmael, a decision that introduced complications into their family dynamics. Sarah's impatience is a common human reaction—we often try to take control when we feel our plans are slipping away.

Their decision to take matters into their own hands features prominently in this narrative. Sarah's doubt about God's promise is underscored when she laughs upon hearing from angels that she will bear a child in her old age (Genesis 18). Her laughter wasn't just a chuckle; it was a reflection of deep-seated skepticism. How often do we brush off God's voice because it doesn't align with our understanding or seem rational at that moment?

But God's promises are steadfast, and He reiterated His covenant to Abraham and specified once again that Sarah herself would bear a son named Isaac. This divine reminder came as a challenge to Sarah's skepticism and served to reinforce God's unchanging plans. It teaches us a critical lesson: when God repeats Himself, it's crucial to listen closely. Often, we might not comprehend His timing, but His promises never fail.

Finally, the long-awaited birth of Isaac brought immense joy and renewed faith for Abraham and Sarah. Against all odds and human logic, Sarah conceived and bore a son—Isaac—fulfilling God's extraordinary promise. The name Isaac, meaning "he will laugh," symbolized not just Sarah's initial doubt but also the joyous fulfillment of God's word. In Genesis 21, Sarah expresses her delight, saying, "God has brought me laughter, and everyone who hears about this will laugh with me" (Genesis 21:6).

Isaac's birth marks a pivotal moment in biblical history. It showcases the beauty and reliability of God's promises, serving as a reminder of His faithfulness. Through this event, Sarah's skeptical laughter transformed into joyful exclamation, demonstrating a profound shift from doubt to trust. The birth of Isaac wasn't just a personal victory for Abraham and Sarah; it was a testament to the transformative power of faith in God's plan.

Abraham's legacy as the father of faith extends beyond his biological descendants. His journey of faith, marked by moments of doubt yet culminating in the fulfilled promise, serves as an example for believers today. Despite the setbacks and the seemingly insurmountable challenges, Abraham's story emphasizes that true faith involves trusting in God's timing, even when the path isn't clear.

This narrative also offers practical lessons for modern-day believers. While waiting, it's natural to experience moments of doubt and uncertainty. However, these moments shouldn't lead us to make hasty decisions that diverge from God's plan. Instead, like Abraham and Sarah, we are encouraged to hold fast to God's promises, confident that His timing is perfect—even if it doesn't align with our own expectations.

Moreover, their story highlights the importance of patience. Waiting on God is not a passive activity; it requires active faith and trust. Abraham and Sarah's experiences remind us that God's timeline often differs from ours, but His fidelity remains constant. Their journey demonstrates that struggles with doubt can coexist with steadfast faith. By examining their lives, we learn that even when our patience wanes and our plans falter, God's promises remain unaffected by our frailties.

Job's Perseverance in Suffering

Job's life was thrown into turmoil by sudden and devastating tragedies. In an instant, his wealth vanished, his children perished, and his health deteriorated, covered from head to toe in painful sores. Despite such overwhelming suffering, Job refused to curse God. His response, "The Lord gave, and the Lord has taken away; blessed be the name of the Lord" (Job 1:21), and "Shall we receive good from God, and shall we not receive evil?" (Job 2:10) highlights his extraordinary strength of character and unwavering faith.

This resilience is even more admirable considering the persistent prodding from his wife, who urged him to curse God and die. Instead of succumbing to despair or turning his back on his faith, Job clung tenaciously to his belief in God's ultimate goodness and sovereignty (Holding on to Your Faith in the Midst of Suffering: Job, 2000). This steadfast faith under pressure became a beacon of hope and inspiration to all around him, showcasing that one's faith can endure even the most severe trials.

As Job's friends entered the scene, their initial attempts at comforting him quickly devolved into an exercise in frustration for Job. They insisted that his suffering must be a direct result of some hidden sin, adhering to a simplistic notion of divine justice—that one is punished solely because they've done wrong. This line of argument only added to Job's distress, offering no genuine comfort or understanding. Job's dialogues with his friends reveal the realistic challenge of waiting for divine answers while feeling deeply misunderstood by those close to you.

In moments of profound pain and uncertainty, it's common for individuals to seek solace in their friends and community. However, Job's experience reminds readers that well-meaning friends can sometimes exacerbate the suffering by offering misguided advice instead of empathetic support. For a believer enduring hardships, it is crucial to remember that one's worth and righteousness are not always reflected in their circumstances. Misunderstandings from others should not shake their trust in God's larger plan.

Eventually, after enduring prolonged silence and endless arguments, God finally speaks to Job out of a whirlwind. Rather than providing direct answers to Job's questions or explaining the reasons behind his suffering, God challenges Job's understanding, revealing the vastness of His wisdom and the complexity of His creation. Through this divine discourse, Job learns humility, recognizing that human beings cannot fully comprehend God's purposes.

This interaction between God and Job is transformative. Job acknowledges his limited perspective and submits to God's greater wisdom. This divine revelation teaches an essential lesson about trust and humility. Believers are reminded to have faith in God's infinite wisdom, even when they do not understand His ways. The realization that not all situations come with clear explanations encourages a stance of humble submission before an omnipotent Creator.

Following this divine encounter, Job experiences restoration. He is blessed even more abundantly than before his trials began. His wealth is doubled, he has more children, and he reaches an old age full of days. This final act in Job's story illustrates the redemptive aspect of faithful waiting. It serves as a powerful testament to the idea that while suffering is a part of the human experience, it does not define one's relationship with God or dictate their future blessings.

Job's journey from deep tragedy through patient endurance to eventual restoration encapsulates the profound truth that waiting upon God, even amidst severe trials, ultimately leads to redemption and blessings. Believers are encouraged to maintain their faith and integrity, regardless of the challenges they face. As Job's life demonstrates, God's timing and plans often surpass human understanding but hold promises of eventual joy and fulfillment.

Job's narrative serves as a rich tapestry interwoven with themes of suffering, patience, faith, and redemption. By examining his story, readers gain insight into how to navigate personal hardships with grace and unwavering faith. They learn that even when life seems insurmountably bleak, holding onto faith can lead to deeper understanding, renewed strength, and ultimate restoration.

In reflecting on Job's interactions with his friends, believers can also glean practical guidelines for supporting others in times of crisis. Effective support involves listening empathetically and offering presence rather than simplistic solutions. Genuine compassion and understanding can provide significant comfort and help reinforce the sufferer's faith during trying times.

The Israelites' Journey to the Promised Land

The journey of the Israelites through the wilderness is one of the most iconic narratives in the Bible, showcasing a profound collective experience of waiting on God's deliverance. Despite being promised freedom from slavery and a land flowing with milk and honey, the Israelites found themselves wandering for 40 long years.

Imagine being caught in what seems like an endless trek, with no clear end in sight. That's exactly how the Israelites felt. God had assured them of their release from Egyptian bondage and a prosperous future in the Promised Land. Yet, instead of quick deliverance, they were met with decades of wandering. This prolonged journey didn't come without reason – it was a divine classroom, albeit a mobile one, designed to teach invaluable lessons.

One of the key reasons for this extended period in the wilderness was the Israelites' repeated doubts and subsequent rebellion against Moses and God. Picture this: you're part of a large caravan traveling together, but every time a challenge arises, complaints ensue. It's hot. Food is scarce. The future looks uncertain. Instead of trusting their leader, many Israelites grumbled and rebelled. They questioned Moses' decisions and doubted God's plan. Their lack of faith led to numerous instances where they tested God's patience.

When you think about it, their behavior isn't entirely foreign to us. How often do we find ourselves questioning life's direction when faced with hardships? The Israelites were no different. Their complaints were loud and frequent – as if grumbling was part of their daily routine. Given the circumstances, it's easy to understand their frustration. However, it's also clear that their recurring disobedience significantly delayed their journey to the Promised Land.

God used this wilderness experience to instill a lesson of dependence on Him. Think of it like boot camp, but with more sand and fewer showers. The desert was unforgiving, yet God provided for the Israelites in miraculous ways. When they were hungry, He sent manna from heaven; when thirsty, water sprang forth from rocks. These daily miracles were not just survival tactics but divine reminders. It's as if God was leaving Post-it notes in the form of miracles saying, "I've got this."

Despite these consistent displays of provision, the Israelites' faith wavered. It became a cycle: doubt, complain, witness a miracle, repeat. But every step of the way, God remained faithful, guiding them with pillars of cloud by day and fire by night.

Alongside provision, guidance was another significant aspect of their wilderness journey. Picture having a GPS that's always accurate, never runs out of battery, and glows both in the daytime and nighttime. The pillar of cloud and pillar of fire served as navigational aids, assuring the Israelites of God's presence and direction. Even when the path seemed unclear or the destination far off, these visual cues acted as constant companions. One would think that such daily divine guidance would bolster unwavering trust, but human nature proved otherwise.

So why did it take so long? Why 40 years for what could have been an 11-day journey? A combination of testing, teaching, and transformation was at play. The wilderness period can be likened to a refining process. God was preparing His people not just to enter a new land but to live in it righteously. It was an extensive formative period, purging ingrained disbelief and cultivating reliance on God.

Finally, after years of trials, learning, and waiting, the Israelites stood at the threshold of the Promised Land. This moment wasn't just the end of their physical journey but also a testament to God's unwavering promise. The land flowing with milk and honey was now within reach, a fulfillment of divine pledge despite the lengthy wait. It's akin to reaching the light at the end of a long, dark tunnel, with the realization that every step in the darkness had a purpose.

While the entire ordeal might seem arduous and prolonged, it encapsulated a unique blend of discipline, faith-building, and ultimate reward. In essence, the story of the Israelites in the wilderness is a powerful metaphor for life's trials and the importance of maintaining faith during periods of uncertainty. It reminds us that waiting on God's timing, though challenging, often leads to outcomes far greater than we could imagine.

Final Thoughts

In this chapter, we've journeyed through some of the Bible's most iconic stories of faithful waiting. From Abraham and Sarah's long quest for a promised child, to Job's perseverance amidst unthinkable suffering, and the Israelites' desert wandering, each tale has shown us that God's timing often comes with lessons and surprises. These biblical figures dealt with doubt and impatience, yet their stories remind us that trusting in God's promises, despite uncertainty, can lead to profound joy and fulfillment.

As we reflect on these narratives, it's clear that waiting is never easy. We've seen how taking matters into our own hands can complicate things, much like Sarah's decision with Hagar. Yet, through trials and tribulations, maintaining faith and patience proved rewarding in the end—whether it's welcoming Isaac, experiencing Job's restoration, or finally reaching the Promised Land. These stories offer not just historical insights but timeless lessons on enduring faith, encouraging us to trust in God's plan, even when the road ahead seems unclear.

Chapter Ten

Maintaining Hope

Maintaining hope when waiting for answers from God can feel like trying to juggle flaming torches while tightrope walking. But this chapter isn't about becoming a circus performer; it's about learning how to keep your spirits up when divine responses seem stuck in heavenly traffic. Picture yourself floating on a sea of uncertainty, clinging to the idea that God's got a plan, even if it feels like He's misplaced His calendar. This chapter is your lifejacket, packed with stories, scriptures, and a splash of humor to keep you buoyant as you navigate the stormy seas of delayed answers.

In our journey through this chapter, you'll dive into biblical gems that act as anchors for your soul, like Hebrews 6:19's vivid imagery of hope as an anchor. We'll also peek at comforting verses such as Jeremiah 29:11, which promises that God has plans for good things, even if they don't align with your current wishlist. Imagine discovering the resilience found in Romans 5:3-5, where suffering surprisingly produces endurance and character. Ah, and there's the ultimate hope booster found in 1 Peter 1:3, where the resurrection offers a living, dynamic hope. Alongside these scriptural insights, we'll share real-life scenarios—from job hunts that resemble epic quests to health battles that feel like running marathons uphill. By the end, you'll have a spiritual toolkit full of practical strategies to nurture and sustain your hope, transforming those anxious wait times into periods of growth and strengthened faith.

Theological Foundations of Hope

Maintaining hope when answers from God seem delayed can feel like an emotional tightrope walk. But the Bible offers us profound theological insights that anchor our hope securely in God's character and promises. Understanding these biblical contexts helps us grasp the essence of hope throughout our journey.

First, let's explore Hebrews 6:19, which describes hope as "an anchor for the soul." This powerful imagery likens hope to an anchor that keeps a ship steady amidst tumultuous seas. Imagine being in a small boat during a storm without an anchor—pretty unnerving, right? Similarly, when life's uncertainties toss us around, hope stabilizes us by keeping us grounded. Our spiritual anchor prevents us from drifting into despair, allowing us to face each wave with confidence that something steadfast holds us firm.

Next, we delve into Jeremiah 29:11: "For I know the plans I have for you, declares the Lord, plans for peace and not for evil, to give you a future and a hope." Now, here's a verse that many people cling to like their favorite comfort food! This promise shows that God has a purpose and a plan for each one of us, even if it doesn't align with our immediate desires or timelines. Think about how architects draft blueprints before starting construction. There's a meticulous plan behind every brick laid, even if the final structure isn't immediately visible. Similarly, trusting this divine blueprint allows us to remain hopeful despite apparent delays.

When Paul writes in Romans 5:3-5, he brings another perspective by stating, "Not only that, but we rejoice in our sufferings, knowing that suffering produces endurance, and endurance produces character, and character produces hope." It's like Paul is saying, "Hey, life's tough, but it builds muscle!" This passage teaches us that suffering is not just random hardship. Instead, it's part of a process that develops endurance, molds character, and ultimately generates hope. Just think about athletes who train rigorously, pushing through pain to build strength and skill. In the same way, our faith muscles grow stronger as we endure life's challenges, nourishing a resilient sense of hope.

Then there's 1 Peter 1:3, which speaks about hope anchored in the resurrection: "Blessed be the God and Father of our Lord Jesus Christ! According to his great mercy, he has caused us to be born again to a living hope through the resurrection of Jesus Christ from the dead." This is the crescendo, folks! The resurrection of Jesus is the ultimate game-changer, offering us a living hope—not a static or fading one. It's like investing in something with guaranteed returns for eternity. This living hope is dynamic and continually renewing, promising us eternal life and victory over death. It elevates our perspective, reminding us that even death can't rob us of the hope found in Christ.

So, let's imagine a real-life scenario. Consider Sarah, who has been praying for years to find a job that aligns with her passions and skills. She feels stuck and wonders if God has forgotten her. When she reads Hebrews 6:19, she's reminded that her hope in God acts as an anchor. Every rejection letter becomes less of a storm and more of a ripple in the water. Sarah clings to the promise in Jeremiah 29:11, understanding that God's plans are greater than the immediate setbacks she faces. Her journey might include suffering, much like Romans 5:3-5 describes, but she recognizes that this ordeal is shaping her endurance and character. Each day, she embraces the living hope of 1 Peter 1:3, fully convinced that God's ultimate plan transcends her current struggles and frustrations.

Another perspective to consider is the story of Joseph in the Old Testament. Betrayed by his brothers, sold into slavery, and imprisoned unjustly, Joseph could have easily succumbed to hopelessness. Yet, his unyielding trust in God's faithfulness kept him anchored. Through relentless trials, his character was honed, and his enduring hope saw eventual fulfillment when he rose to become a powerful leader in Egypt. His journey reflects the transformative power of hope grounded in divine promises.

Modern-day examples abound, too. Take someone dealing with a chronic illness. Every doctor's appointment might feel like yet another wave crashing against their little boat. They might turn to Hebrews 6:19 and hold onto the anchor of hope, trusting God's steadfastness when their strength wanes. By reflecting on Jeremiah 29:11, they remember that even in their suffering, God's plan includes a future filled with hope. Romans 5:3-5 reassures them that this journey, fraught with pain, will produce perseverance and, in turn, deepen their hope. The reality of 1 Peter 1:3 assures them that their ultimate healing lies in the resurrection promise, giving purpose and meaning beyond their present discomfort.

Reflecting on these scriptures reminds us that hope is not passive wishful thinking; it's an active engagement with God's promises. As we experience life's storms—whether waiting for a job, dealing with health issues, or grappling with personal relationships—we need to anchor our hope in God's unchanging character and His faithful assurances. This hope transforms our waiting into a period of growth, our suffering into a catalyst for perseverance, and our faith into a beacon of light for others navigating their own turbulent seas.

Daily Habits to Nurture Hope

Establishing the Practice of Morning Affirmations Focused on God's Promises

Imagine starting each day with a spark of positivity, a sense of purpose, and a reminder of God's unwavering promises. Morning affirmations can do just that. They are simple, yet powerful statements that can reshape our mindset and strengthen our faith. For example, repeating phrases like "I am loved by God," or "God's plans for me are good" can set a hopeful tone for the day. These affirmations remind us of the spiritual truths we often overlook amidst daily chaos.

Morning affirmations don't have to be grand declarations. They can be as simple as acknowledging God's presence and expressing trust in His timing. Write them down and place them where you'll see them first thing—on your nightstand, bathroom mirror, or even as a screen-saver on your phone. Incorporate scripture into your affirmations to ground them in divine truth. (Excel Still More, 2019) suggests using Bible verses such as Jeremiah 29:11: "For I know the plans I have for you," declares the Lord, "plans to prosper you and not to harm you, plans to give you hope and a future." Such verses can reinforce our faith in God's promises and keep us anchored.

Encouraging the Habit of Expressing Gratitude Daily to Recognize God's Blessings

Gratitude is like a lens through which we view life more clearly, spotting blessings we might otherwise miss. Developing a habit of expressing gratitude can shift our focus from what we lack to what we have, fostering a hopeful outlook. Start a gratitude journal and jot down three things you're thankful for each day. This practice takes only a few minutes but can dramatically change your perspective.

It's not about listing extravagant blessings; even small things count. Thank God for a good night's sleep, a warm cup of coffee, or a kind gesture from a neighbor. As we acknowledge these everyday gifts, we become more aware of God's continuous provision. Writing down specific instances amplifies the impact. For example, instead of writing, "I'm thankful for my family," you could say, "I'm grateful for the laughter around the dinner table last night." This specificity makes gratitude tangible and real.

Expressing gratitude also extends beyond journaling. Verbally thanking others for their positive actions can uplift both parties. Sharing your appreciation with friends and family nurtures an atmosphere of mutual respect and love, reflecting God's work in your life.

Integrating Consistent Prayer Time to Seek Guidance While Maintaining a Hopeful Perspective

Consistent prayer—a dialogue with God—nurtures our relationship with Him and aligns our hearts with His will. It's essential to carve out regular time for prayer, turning it into a daily ritual rather than a sporadic event. Choose a time that suits your routine, whether it's early in the morning, during lunch breaks, or before bed.

Prayer is not just about requests; it's also about listening and reflecting. Begin with praise, acknowledging God's greatness. Move on to thanksgiving, then present your needs and concerns. Finally, take a moment to listen. Silence in prayer can be uncomfortable but often holds profound revelations.

Maintaining a hopeful perspective through prayer means trusting God's answers, even if they seem delayed. Recall Hannah's story in 1 Samuel. She prayed fervently for a child and remained hopeful despite years of waiting. Her perseverance in prayer eventually led to the birth of Samuel, demonstrating that God's timing is always perfect.

Incorporating scriptural promises into your prayers can bolster your hope. When you feel anxious, pray Philippians 4:6-7: "Do not be anxious about anything, but in every situation, by prayer and petition, with thanksgiving, present your requests to God. And the peace of God, which transcends all understanding, will guard your hearts and your minds in Christ Jesus." This verse reassures us that God hears our prayers and offers peace amid uncertainty.

Finding Fellowship with Groups That Encourage Hope and Share Testimonies

We are social beings, and community plays a pivotal role in sustaining hope. Surrounding ourselves with people who uplift and inspire us can significantly boost our resilience. Joining a fellowship group provides a supportive environment where shared experiences and testimonies fortify collective faith.

A great fellowship group isn't just about attending meetings; it's about building relationships. Look for groups that not only study scripture but also share personal stories of God's faithfulness. Hearing how others have navigated difficult times can encourage you in your journey.

For instance, many churches offer small group sessions or Bible studies where members discuss how they're applying biblical principles in their lives. This setup allows for intimate interactions and deeper connections. Within these groups, sharing testimonies becomes a source of collective strength. Knowing that someone else has faced similar challenges and emerged victorious can provide immense hope.

Additionally, online communities offer another avenue for fellowship, especially for those with busy schedules or limited physical access to church groups. Platforms like Facebook or Zoom host virtual Bible studies and prayer meetings, making it easier to connect with like-minded individuals.

While the primary aim is spiritual growth, remember to infuse a bit of fun into these gatherings. Hosting potlucks, game nights, or outings can create lasting bonds and make the journey of faith enjoyable and enriching.

Creating a Balanced Routine for Hope-Filled Living

Balancing these practices—morning affirmations, gratitude journaling, prayer, and fellowship—is key to sustaining hope. Each one complements the others, creating a holistic approach to nurturing faith. Start by assessing your current routine and identifying gaps where these habits can fit.

Perhaps you can begin your day with affirmations during breakfast, jot down gratitude notes at lunch, spend time in prayer after work, and attend fellowship gatherings weekly. The aim is to integrate these practices seamlessly into your life, making them second nature over time.

Remember, the goal is not perfection but progress. Some days will be easier than others, and that's okay. What's important is your commitment to cultivating an environment where hope thrives. By consistently practicing these habits, you build a strong foundation that can withstand life's storms.

Creating Vision Boards or Spiritual Reminders

Maintaining hope during periods of waiting can be incredibly challenging, but one effective strategy to stay focused and motivated is to visually represent your hopes and prayers. Visual tools like vision boards can play a pivotal role in this journey by providing constant reminders of your spiritual aspirations and goals.

Let's start with the concept of vision boards. Vision boards are physical or digital collages that depict images, words, and quotes that represent your dreams and aspirations. They serve as visual representations of what you are hoping for and praying about. By having a tangible reminder of your hopes, you keep your focus on God's promises rather than on the frustrations of delay. While some critics argue that vision boards may lean towards self-centeredness, they can actually be an excellent tool for manifesting spiritual aspirations if used correctly. To ensure that our vision boards align with our faith, it's important to ground them in biblical truths.

One way to make your vision board spiritually enriching is by incorporating biblical verses and images that resonate with God's promises. Adding scriptures that remind you of God's faithfulness not only

grounds your vision board in divine truth but also continually reinforces His promises to you. For example, including verses like Jeremiah
29:11, which talks about God's plans to prosper you and give you
hope, can be extremely uplifting. Images that depict scenes from the
Bible, such as Jesus walking on water or the serene landscapes of the
Holy Land, can serve as powerful reminders of God's presence in
your life. By surrounding yourself with such imagery and text, you
immerse yourself in a spiritual atmosphere that nurtures hope and
faith. (Noble, 2020).

Physical reminders also play a crucial role in maintaining hope daily.
Sticky notes with encouraging words placed around your home, office,
or even in your car can serve as quick boosts of optimism throughout your day. Digital reminders set on your phone or computer can
prompt you to take a moment to pray or reflect on God's promises.
These small actions create a continuous thread of hope that runs
through your daily routine, keeping you anchored even when distractions abound. Moreover, these reminders help you shift focus from
immediate anxieties to the bigger picture of God's plan for your life.

Another impactful approach is to engage in group activities to create
collective vision boards reflecting shared hopes and prayers. Coming
together with friends, family, or members of your faith community to
create a communal vision board can be both enjoyable and spiritually
enriching. This activity fosters a sense of unity and shared purpose,
reinforcing the collective faith and hope within the group. Imagine
sitting down with loved ones, sharing stories of what you hope for, and
collectively praying over each other's dreams as you create your vision
boards. The experience becomes more than just crafting; it turns into
a spiritual exercise of mutual encouragement and support. In times of
waiting, knowing that others stand with you in prayer and share your

hopes can significantly bolster your spirit. (How a Vision Board Can Help You Reach Your Goals for 2022, 2020).

It's important to note that creating a vision board isn't just about pasting random pictures onto a poster. There needs to be intentionality behind every image and word chosen. Start by praying and asking God to reveal His plans and promises for your life. Allow His guidance to inform what you place on your vision board. This ensures that your focus remains aligned with His will rather than drifting toward worldly desires. Every time you look at your vision board, you're reminded not just of what you want, but of what God has promised you.

In addition to vision boards, setting daily reminders plays a critical role in nurturing hope. Simple acts such as placing sticky notes with inspirational quotes or scriptures in frequent places like your bathroom mirror, kitchen fridge, or work desk can create multiple touchpoints of encouragement throughout your day. You could also set digital reminders on your phone to prompt you to pause and reflect on a particular scripture or promise. This practice helps in constantly realigning your thoughts with God's promises and maintaining a hopeful outlook. For instance, receiving a notification that says, "God's timing is perfect," during a stressful moment can immediately shift your focus back to trusting Him.

Collective vision boards extend beyond personal benefits; they foster communal bonds and collective strength. Organizing group sessions where families, friends, or church groups come together to create vision boards can amplify the sense of shared hope. These sessions can be filled with laughter, discussions, and prayers, making the experience rich and memorable. When everyone lays out their personal hopes and prayers and sees them visually represented alongside those of their peers, it creates a tapestry of shared dreams, bound by faith and mutual encouragement.

Making a vision board can also be a family activity, involving children and teenagers. Teaching kids to set their own goals and visualize their dreams is a valuable lesson in faith and perseverance. It instills in them the importance of dreaming big and trusting God with their futures. Plus, the creative process can be a fun and interactive way for younger family members to engage with biblical teachings and understand the power of hope.

Bringing It All Together

We've danced through some profound theological insights, discovering how hope can act as an anchor for our souls amid life's storms. From the image of a sturdy ship surviving tumultuous seas to the promise of divine blueprints guiding our lives, we've uncovered a treasure trove of biblical wisdom. Each scripture, be it Paul's robust encouragements about suffering producing endurance or Peter's proclamation of living hope through resurrection, gives us solid footing when answers seem delayed. These ancient words transform our waiting into active engagement, nurturing optimism and resilience.

Remember Sarah and Joseph? Their stories echo the powerful message that trusting in God's promises becomes a beacon of light during challenging times. Sarah's job search and Joseph's roller-coaster life remind us that amidst rejection letters and unjust imprisonments, hope anchored in faith keeps us steady. As you weave these practices into your daily routine—whether it's morning affirmations, gratitude journaling, or sharing testimonies with fellow believers—you create a balanced, hope-filled life. So, buckle up, grab your spiritual anchor, and sail confidently through life's stormy waters, assured that there's a divine promise holding you firm.

Chapter Eleven

Handling Disappointment

Navigating moments of disappointment can be like trying to find your way out of a corn maze with no map and an overcast sky. It's tricky, frustrating, and sometimes you just want to plop down and call it a day. But take heart; you're not alone in this sticky situation. Throughout the ages, countless people have faced setbacks and gut-punch disappointments, particularly during those long periods of waiting on God. The Bible is chock-full of stories featuring folks who felt the sting of disappointment yet managed to come out stronger on the other side. Their journeys are rife with lessons in emotional resilience, faith, and practical approaches that might just help you cope with your own hiccups and hurdles.

In this chapter, we'll dive into these biblical narratives to uncover some gold nuggets of wisdom. You'll read about Job's unshakeable faith despite losing almost everything, David's raw honesty with God in his darkest hours, and Elijah's bout with burnout followed by gentle divine care. We won't stop there; we'll also examine how Jesus himself handled excruciating disappointment in Gethsemane. Through these stories, you'll gain insights into how pouring out your heart can lead to healing, why sometimes resting and listening for that still, small voice is essential, and the importance of leaning on trusted companions during tough times. By the end of this chapter, you'll have a toolkit of emotional resilience strategies grounded in ancient wisdom but entirely applicable to today's challenges.

Biblical Responses to Disappointment

Amidst the swirling clouds of disappointment, biblical figures offer profound lessons and encouragement that align with our own experiences. Take Job, for instance. Picture this: a man stripped of nearly everything—his wealth, his health, even his children—yet he stands firm in his faith. His story serves as an impeccable lesson in resilience. Though he questions God intensely, demanding answers to the "why" of his suffering, he never relinquishes his faith. His friends come up with all sorts of simplistic explanations, but Job's unwavering faith turns out to be the essence of his journey. In the end, God responds to Job not with clear answers but with questions that elevate his understanding to appreciate the mystery and grandeur of divine creation. This narrative encourages us to shift our focus from seeking specific answers to trusting in God's wisdom, even during inexplicable suffering (Yancey, 2023).

Now, let's mosey over to David, who was no stranger to the gut-wrenching pangs of disappointment. Through his psalms, David wears his emotions on his sleeve, giving voice to his feelings of abandonment, fear, and despair. Imagine him in Psalm 22, crying out, "My God, my God, why have you forsaken me?" These aren't just cries of desperation but acts of faith. By laying bare his raw emotions before God, David reveals a relationship that tolerates complexities—doubts, fears, and even anger. His honesty doesn't undermine his faith; it strengthens it. He shows us that vocalizing our struggles can lead to clarity and healing, breaking the cycle of bottled-up frustrations. So, next time you're feeling like a pressure cooker ready to blow, take a page out of David's book and let it out.

Elijah's tale is another gem worth mentioning. After a blazing victory on Mount Carmel, where fire rained down from heaven, you'd think he'd be riding high. But nope! Elijah plummets into deep despair, fleeing into the wilderness and basically saying, "God, I've had enough. Just take my life." It's burnout, pure and simple. God's response is gently multifaceted: He provides food, allows Elijah to rest, and then speaks to him not in a great wind or earthquake but in a gentle whisper. This teaches us about the necessity of seeking God's presence and taking physical and emotional rest when burnout looms large. When the world's weight presses down, sometimes what we need isn't a dramatic intervention but tender care and a new sense of purpose.

And then we have Jesus in Gethsemane. Here's the Son of God, sweating drops of blood, overwhelmed with sorrow to the point of death. He prays, "Father, if it's possible, let this cup pass from me," yet ultimately, he submits to God's will. This moment highlights the human experience of disappointment, showing that even Jesus grappled with it. The scene also underscores the value of seeking companionship in prayer. Jesus didn't go through this ordeal alone; he took Peter, James, and John with him. Although they fell asleep (not exactly the best support crew), His intention was clear: there's value in having others around during our darkest hours. When facing life's Gethsemane moments, reaching out for companionship and shared prayer can provide immense solace and strength.

In all these stories, one overarching theme is evident: the Bible isn't shy about tackling the reality of pain and the complexity of human emotions. Instead, it provides a framework where suffering is acknowledged, and honest expressions of doubt and fear are part of a vibrant faith. The narratives of Job, David, Elijah, and Jesus show that disappointment and suffering are integral parts of the human condition, but so is the Divine presence amid those trials. There are no easy answers or shortcuts, but there's always the assurance of God's enduring presence and unfailing love.

So, the next time you find yourself sinking in the mud of disappointment, consider the biblical perspective. Like Job, dare to lift your eyes beyond your present suffering, trusting in something greater. Like David, pour out your heart, knowing that honesty and faith can coexist. Like Elijah, seek rest and listen for that still, small voice guiding you forward. And like Jesus, allow yourself the comfort of trusted companions and surrender the situation into God's hands.

Reframing Setbacks as Opportunities

When life throws us curveballs, it's easy to feel overwhelmed and discouraged. However, setbacks can be more than mere obstacles; they can be transformative opportunities for growth and moments of divine guidance. Let's explore how some biblical figures turned their disappointments into stepping stones for greatness and how you can do the same during your waiting period.

Consider Joseph's journey from being a betrayed brother to becoming a leader in Egypt. Joseph's brothers were envious of him and sold him into slavery. As if that wasn't enough, he was later falsely accused and imprisoned. From an outsider's perspective, Joseph's life seemed like one long string of unfortunate events. But Joseph never lost faith in God's plan. In prison, he utilized his God-given talents to interpret dreams, eventually gaining favor with Pharaoh. Joseph was elevated to a position of power, where he not only rescued Egypt from famine but also reunited with his family. This incredible turnaround illustrates how setbacks can pave the way for significant blessings when we remain faithful and open to divine guidance.

Moses' story offers another valuable lesson about the power of waiting. After fleeing Egypt, Moses spent forty years in the wilderness before returning to lead the Israelites out of slavery. During this time, he wasn't just twiddling his thumbs; Moses was learning invaluable lessons in leadership and character. He went from a man who felt unworthy to speak to Pharaoh to someone who confidently led millions of people through seemingly insurmountable challenges. The wilderness was God's training ground for Moses, equipping him with patience, humility, and resilience—qualities essential for his monumental task ahead. Waiting periods are fertile grounds for personal development, teaching us virtues we may lack and preparing us for future responsibilities.

Paul's imprisonment shines light on yet another perspective. Rather than viewing his confinement as a barrier, Paul saw it as an opportunity to further his mission. While under house arrest, he wrote several letters that became pivotal parts of the New Testament. These letters provided spiritual guidance and encouragement to early Christians, spreading the Gospel far and wide. Paul's imprisonment teaches us that limitations don't have to hinder our purpose. Instead, they can drive us to find innovative ways to achieve our goals, proving that our spirit can flourish even in restrictive circumstances.

The transformative power of trials isn't limited to biblical stories. Real-life testimonies echo these timeless truths, revealing how communal support and mindset shifts can turn disappointment into community-building opportunities. Take Sarah, for example, who faced career setbacks and felt isolated. She joined a local support group, opening up about her struggles and finding solace in shared experiences. Through mutual encouragement and collective wisdom, Sarah discovered new passions and opportunities she hadn't considered before. What began as a personal setback blossomed into a vibrant community initiative, fostering collaboration and growth among its members.

Similarly, John's story emphasizes the importance of shifting perspectives during challenging times. After a debilitating injury sidelined his athletic career, John initially wallowed in despair. But with the help of friends and mentors, he started focusing on what he could still achieve instead of what he had lost. He became involved in adaptive sports, mentoring others facing similar challenges. His experience underscores that our trials can uniquely qualify us to help others, turning personal disappointment into avenues for broader impact and fulfillment.

These narratives teach us crucial lessons about handling disappointment. They remind us that setbacks don't signify failure but rather opportunities for growth and divine intervention. When we approach our challenges with faith, resilience, and an openness to learn, we can transform our disappointments into milestones of success and spiritual maturity.

Understanding that setbacks are part of a larger divine plan can bring comfort and direction. Just as Joseph's betrayal led him to save nations, and Moses' wilderness years prepared him for leadership, your current struggles can serve a higher purpose. It's essential to maintain a positive outlook and seek God's guidance during these times. Remember, every great story of triumph has moments of hardship that shaped the protagonist's journey.

Emotional Resilience in the Face of Delay

Handling disappointment while waiting on God's timing can feel like trying to stay afloat in a turbulent sea. We often find ourselves weighed down by uncertainty and longing for the shore of fulfillment. Developing emotional resilience during these times is crucial for maintaining faith and a positive outlook, so let's dive into some practical strategies that can help.

One powerful tool to shift our focus from what we lack to what we already have is maintaining a gratitude journal. Imagine starting your day recognizing the blessings that are present in your life—big or small. This practice doesn't require any special skills; just grab a notebook and jot down a few things you're grateful for each day. You might be surprised at how this simple act can transform your perspective. Research shows that those who consistently practice gratitude tend to experience fewer symptoms of depression and greater overall well-being (Kehl, 2024). When we make it a habit to focus on the positives, even if they seem insignificant, we're training our minds to look for the silver lining, which can greatly enhance our emotional resilience during challenging times.

Now, let's talk about incorporating mindfulness practices with prayer. Think of mindfulness as a way to anchor yourself in the present moment without judgment. When combined with prayer, it becomes a powerful duo that cultivates peace and helps manage anxiety. Start with a few minutes of deep breathing to center your mind before you pray. Allow yourself to be fully present in your conversation with God, laying your worries at His feet. Mindfulness and meditation can improve emotional awareness, making it easier to navigate through periods of uncertainty calmly. For example, taking five minutes in the morning to sit quietly and focus on your breath can set a peaceful tone for the rest of your day.

Building supportive relationships within your faith community serves as another cornerstone of emotional resilience. Picture yourself in the company of fellow believers who uplift and encourage you. These relationships offer shared support during tough times, reminding you that you're not alone on this journey. Maybe it's participating in a small group where you can share your struggles and triumphs or finding a prayer partner who checks in regularly. Strengthening these bonds can provide a buffer against the storms of disappointment. It's like having a network of anchors that keep you grounded when waves of doubt try to pull you under.

Don't underestimate the power of setting small, achievable goals. When you're stuck in what feels like an endless waiting period, it's easy to become disheartened. By setting and accomplishing small goals, you create a sense of progress and forward movement. Think of this strategy as building a ladder out of a pit—each rung represents a small goal achieved, helping you climb out little by little. Perhaps you decide to read a chapter of a book each week, take daily walks, or learn a new skill. These actions, though seemingly minor, build momentum and foster self-compassion. They serve as reminders that you're moving forward, even if the bigger picture is still unfolding.

But let's also address the elephant in the room—sometimes, despite our best efforts, the weight of disappointment feels overwhelming. It's crucial to recognize these moments and extend grace to ourselves. Acknowledge your feelings without judgment and remember that it's okay to seek help when needed. Reaching out to a mental health professional or a trusted mentor can provide additional support and strategies tailored to your specific circumstances. Just as we wouldn't hesitate to see a doctor for a physical ailment, seeking emotional and spiritual guidance is a proactive step toward holistic well-being.

Final Thoughts

In this chapter, we've delved into the stories of Job, David, Elijah, and Jesus, uncovering how they navigated through their darkest moments. Each story serves as a reminder that feeling disappointed or frustrated is part of the human experience. Yet, by embracing honesty in our emotions, seeking rest, and leaning on trusted companions, we can find strength and resilience. The biblical narratives show us that it's okay to question, to feel deeply, and to seek support, all while maintaining our faith.

Now, turning points aren't just for drama series or epic novels—they happen in real life too! Whether it's learning from Joseph's journey from a pit to a palace, Moses' wilderness bootcamp, or Paul's prison epistle marathon, setbacks often set the stage for incredible transformations. By reframing our challenges as opportunities for growth and divine guidance, and by practicing gratitude, mindfulness, and building supportive relationships, we're better equipped to face life's curveballs. So next time you're pacing the waiting room of life, remember: every setback is just a plot twist in your grander story, bringing you one step closer to personal and spiritual triumph.

Chapter Twelve

Integrating Waiting into Worship

I ntegrating waiting into worship might sound a bit like suggesting you add broccoli to your favorite dessert—unusual at first glance, but surprisingly beneficial. In our world of instant everything—from coffee to gratification—learning the art of waiting doesn't just deepen spirituality; it adds unforeseen layers of resilience and understanding. Imagine turning off the noise, hitting the pause button on life's chaos, and giving silence a chance to speak volumes. This chapter dares you to slow down, chill out, and discover that spiritual growth often happens not in the rush, but in the wait.

So what can you expect from this dive into divine downtime? For starters, we'll explore reflective worship practices that prioritize patience over speed. Think structured silences, guided reflections, and worship songs that echo themes of hope and perseverance. Then we'll sprinkle a few practical tips on incorporating these elements seamlessly into your worship routine. Alongside this, you'll uncover the beauty of collective waiting moments and find inventive ways to visually remind yourself—and others—that God's timing is always spot-on. Buckle up—or better yet, unbuckle and get comfy—we're about to embark on a journey where waiting takes center stage.

Worship practices that emphasize waiting

In today's world, where instant gratification is often the norm, reflective worship practices can be a refreshing change that encourages individuals to embrace an attitude of waiting. This approach challenges our fast-paced culture and provides a path to slow down, refocus, and recognize God's presence in the silence. Reflective worship involves creating space for silence and stillness within the service, allowing congregants to pause and meditate on God's word and their relationship with Him.

Consider starting your worship service with a moment of quiet reflection. This could involve reading a short scripture passage followed by a period of silence, inviting everyone to contemplate the message and its relevance to their lives. By doing so, you provide a stark contrast to the constant noise and busyness that often pervades modern life. It helps individuals center themselves, clear their minds of distractions, and open their hearts to what God is conveying (Riggs, 2019).

A poignant way to facilitate this is through guided reflections. Encourage the congregation to reflect privately on specific themes, such as gratitude, patience, or trust. These moments don't need to be lengthy; even a few minutes of silence can create a powerful impact. Over time, this practice fosters a sense of expectancy and receptivity to

God's guidance, emphasizing that waiting is not just passive idleness but an active engagement in spiritual growth.

In addition to reflective periods, incorporating songs of waiting can further solidify the theme. Music has a unique ability to express emotions that words alone may struggle to convey. Selecting worship songs that focus on themes of waiting, hope, and trust can remind attendees that they are not alone in their struggles. These songs can resonate deeply, fostering a communal experience that unites individuals in their shared journeys of faith.

When selecting these songs, consider the lyrics carefully. Look for compositions that speak directly to the human experience of waiting—those moments of uncertainty and yearning for God's intervention. Songs like "While I'm Waiting" by John Waller or "Everlasting God" by Chris Tomlin are excellent examples that address themes of perseverance and reliance on God's timing. By incorporating such music into the worship routine, you help reinforce the message that waiting is an integral part of spiritual life, woven into the fabric of worship.

Scheduled waiting moments during services can also play a critical role in teaching the congregation about the value of patience and reflection. Designating specific times for collective waiting emphasizes the importance of pausing and aligning hearts with God. One practical guideline is to incorporate a brief period of silent prayer or meditation after each major element of the worship service, such as following a song, a scripture reading, or a sermon segment.

These intentional pauses can serve multiple functions: they allow the congregation to internalize what they've just experienced, give space for the Holy Spirit to move, and prevent the service from feeling rushed. To implement this effectively, communicate the purpose of these pauses clearly to the congregation. Explain that these moments are designed for personal reflection, prayer, and connection with God. Over time, these pauses will become a cherished part of the worship experience, providing attendees with a regular opportunity to practice waiting and listening for God's voice.

Utilizing visual elements in worship can greatly enhance the experience and provide tangible reminders of God's timing. Visual aids, such as symbols of waiting, can be seamlessly integrated into the worship environment to underscore the theme. For instance, consider using imagery of seeds, which capture the essence of growth and patience. Seeds must be planted, nurtured, and given time to grow—much like our faith and understanding of God's plan.

Another effective visual could be a clock or hourglass displayed prominently in the worship space. These symbols serve as constant reminders that God's timing is different from ours and that there is beauty and purpose in the waiting. Additionally, incorporating time-lapse videos showing natural processes, like flowers blooming or the changing of seasons, can visually illustrate how beautiful things unfold when given the necessary time.

To further engage the congregation, invite members to contribute to these visual elements. They could write prayers or thoughts related to their personal experiences with waiting and pin them to a designated prayer board. This participatory approach not only makes the waiting theme more interactive but also fosters a sense of community as individuals see that others share similar journeys.

Praying through periods of uncertainty

In a world that continually moves at breakneck speed, the act of waiting can feel painfully counterintuitive. Yet, it is within these moments of pause that we often find the most profound spiritual growth. This section explores how incorporating prayer into our waiting periods can transform our experience, emphasizing God's unwavering faithfulness.

Adopting Prayers of Ascent can be an incredibly powerful tool. The Psalms, particularly those known as the Songs of Ascents, provide vivid expressions of human emotion ranging from desperation to hope. Think about Psalm 121 which begins with, "I lift up my eyes to the mountains—where does my help come from?" When you feel stuck in a prolonged period of waiting, echoing these prayers can help articulate your feelings and remind you that many have walked this path before you. By connecting your experiences with biblical examples, you create a bridge between your present struggles and the timeless wisdom found in scripture. These prayers serve as both a comfort and a guide, showing you that waiting is not a void but a vital part of your spiritual journey (Psalms of Ascent — Blog 1 | GCD, 2014).

While individual prayer is essential, Praying in Community adds another layer of support. Imagine you're sitting in a circle with fellow believers, each taking turns to voice their own periods of waiting and uncertainty. It's like group therapy, but with a divine twist. When everyone comes together in prayer during worship gatherings, it transforms individual waiting into communal resilience. You are no longer isolated in your struggles; instead, you are buoyed by the collective empathy and support of your community. This kind of prayer fosters a sense of belonging and shared burden, reinforcing that you are not alone in your journey.

Written Prayers offer another avenue for navigating the emotional landscape of waiting. Writing down your prayers forces you to slow down and truly reflect on what you're experiencing. It's like journaling but with a focus on dialogue with God. Take, for instance, the practice of creating written prayers centered around waiting. You might write about your hopes, frustrations, and any insights you gain during this time. Over time, these written prayers become a tangible record of God's faithfulness. Whenever doubt creeps in, you can look back at these pages and see all the ways God has been present, even when you felt He was silent. It's an exercise in patience and trust, both virtues that the act of waiting naturally cultivates.

Lastly, let's talk about Prayer Walks. This practice bridges the gap between physical movement and spiritual stillness. Imagine walking through a park, each step acting as a rhythm of a prayer. The act of moving helps connect body, mind, and spirit. Nature itself becomes a classroom where God teaches lessons on timing and patience. As you walk, you might observe how trees grow slowly over time or how seasons change methodically. These observations serve as metaphors for your own journey, reminding you that God's timing is perfect even if it doesn't align with your personal schedule.

So, there you have it—four powerful ways to integrate prayer into your waiting periods, each offering a unique approach to engaging with God during these challenging times. Whether you're adopting Prayers of Ascent, joining in communal prayers, crafting written reflections, or embarking on prayer walks, each method provides a pathway to understanding God's faithfulness more deeply.

Including waiting themes in personal devotions

Incorporating the theme of waiting into one's devotional practices can be a transformative experience. It provides space for personal reflection, growth, and deep connection with God's timing. By integrating specific activities and exercises focused on waiting, individuals can cultivate patience and trust in God's plan, especially during periods of uncertainty.

To start, embracing daily reflections centered around waiting is an excellent way to incorporate this theme into your spiritual routine. During these moments, take time to acknowledge your current circumstances openly. Reflect on how waiting plays a role in your life's daily events. Consider the ways that scripture speaks to waiting, and allow these passages to speak into your situation. This practice helps you connect with biblical teachings about God's timing and align your heart with His plans, rather than your own timeline.

For instance, consider setting aside a few minutes each day to meditate on verses like Psalm 27:14, which says, "Wait for the Lord; be strong, and let your heart take courage; wait for the Lord!" Reflecting on such scriptures not only grounds you in faith but also encourages resilience—something that becomes particularly valuable when life seems unpredictable. You may also find it helpful to write down your thoughts during these reflections, turning them into a form of daily journaling.

Moving on to Scripture memorization, this practice can deepen your understanding and trust in God's promises. When you memorize verses related to waiting, like Isaiah 40:31 ("But they who wait for the Lord shall renew their strength..."), these words become ingrained in your mind and heart. They serve as a constant reminder of God's faithfulness and His perfect timing. Over time, this practice builds a strong foundation of trust, allowing these truths to surface naturally whenever feelings of impatience or doubt arise.

Memorizing scripture doesn't have to be a daunting task. Start small by choosing one verse each week. Write it on a card or post-it note and place it somewhere you'll see it frequently—like on your bathroom mirror or refrigerator door. Recite it throughout the day, letting its message sink into your spirit. As you commit more verses to memory, you'll find that they begin to shape your reactions and attitudes, providing peace and assurance in times of waiting.

Creating a gratitude journal is another powerful tool for embedding themes of waiting into your devotional practices. Waiting can often be accompanied by anxiety and frustration, but a gratitude journal shifts your focus towards appreciation and recognition of your blessings. Each day, write down things you're thankful for—even the small, seemingly insignificant ones. This act of recording your blessings can be quite revealing; it highlights God's provision and care in the midst of waiting.

Through this practice, you'll start to notice patterns in your life where God has been faithful, even when things didn't happen according to your timing. The simple act of writing down what you're grateful for forces you to slow down and recognize the good things around you. It's an exercise in mindfulness that brings your attention back to God's faithfulness, reinforcing the idea that He knows best and His timing is perfect.

Engaging in artistic expressions can also provide a therapeutic re-lease and enhance your connection with God while waiting. Whether through painting, drawing, music, or another creative outlet, express-ing themes of waiting artistically allows you to explore and understand your feelings in a non-verbal way. It taps into the emotional com-plexities of waiting, offering insights that might be difficult to access through words alone.

For example, you might create a piece of art that represents a season of waiting in your life. Maybe it's a painting of a tree in winter, barren but full of potential for spring. Or perhaps you write poetry or songs that capture the tension between longing and trusting. These artistic endeavors can serve as both a form of worship and a means of process-ing your emotions. They provide a unique way to communicate with God and reflect on His presence in your life.

The beauty of incorporating artistic expressions is that there are no right or wrong ways to do it. It's a personal experience that allows you to bring your whole self into the act of waiting. As you engage creatively, you may find that new layers of understanding and con-nection with God open up, helping you navigate the waiting periods with greater grace and insight.

Bringing It All Together

Incorporating the art of waiting into your worship practices and daily walk with God might seem out of sync with our instant-gratification culture, but it's a game-changer for deepening your spiritual jour-ney. Reflective worship, guided reflections, and moments of silence encourage us to pause and connect more fully with God's presence. By embracing silence and stillness, we can meditate on His word and cultivate a sense of expectancy for His guidance. It's like hitting the spiritual refresh button—suddenly, you're no longer rushing through life, but taking the time to truly listen to what God has to say.

Moreover, adding elements like songs of waiting and visual aids makes waiting a communal yet deeply personal experience. You're not just waiting on your own; you're surrounded by a community that shares the same journey, enhancing your resilience and faith. Visual symbols like seeds or hourglasses remind us that growth and understanding flourish over time. So, whether it's through singing, silence, or setting up a prayer board, these practices teach us that waiting is an active part of worship and spiritual growth. In this fast-paced world, learning to wait might just be the secret ingredient to a richer, more fulfilled spiritual life.

Chapter Thirteen

Celebrating Fulfillment

Recognizing and celebrating the fulfillment of God's promises is much like throwing a surprise party for your soul. Imagine waiting for that big reveal, the moment when all those prayers and hopes finally come to fruition. When it happens, it's like unwrapping a long-anticipated gift—joyful, surprising, and deeply satisfying. Just as you'd cherish an unexpected but perfect present, recognizing God's faithfulness brings about a profound sense of gratitude and wonderment. It's not just about acknowledging the end result but also savoring the journey that got you there, with all its twists, turns, and divine interventions.

In this chapter, we'll reflect on how journaling can anchor these moments in our memory, turning each fulfilled promise into a milestone of faith. We'll explore the power of sharing your story within a community, transforming isolated experiences into collective celebrations. We'll dive into practical ways to create tangible reminders of God's faithfulness, like memory boxes filled with keepsakes of answered prayers. By integrating these practices, you'll discover how they transform your spiritual journey, making each fulfilled promise not just a moment of joy but a lasting testament to God's unwavering love and commitment. This exploration will leave you equipped to recognize and celebrate each of God's promises, both big and small, with renewed appreciation and heartfelt gratitude.

Reflecting on the Journey Post-Waiting

Reflecting on the journey of waiting is like finally finding that missing sock behind the dryer: enlightening, sometimes surprising, but ultimately satisfying. When we pause to reflect, we can better appreciate how far we've come and the bumps we encountered along the way. This isn't simply looking back nostalgically; it's about identifying growth and recognizing God's hand during times of uncertainty.

Think about those moments when life felt like a suspenseful movie, and you weren't sure what was around the corner. Reflection helps solidify our experiences, turning those fuzzy memories into clear milestones. By reflecting, we recognize how we've changed and grown, even if at the time it felt like we were running in place. The ultimate plot twist? Realizing that God was there the whole time, guiding us through every loop and detour.

One powerful way to ensure that these reflections stick is through journaling. Now, I know what you're thinking—journals are for teenage angst and doodles of crushes, right? Wrong! Journaling your thoughts creates a personal history of faith. It's like having a secret weapon against doubt, capturing God's movement and patterns of faithfulness over time. Plus, it can serve as a guidebook when you face future uncertainties. Imagine flipping through pages filled with "aha" moments, answered prayers, and even those "what was I thinking?" entries. Each word acts as a testament to God's unwavering presence in your life.

Journaling isn't just a solitary activity—it can also be a springboard for community connections. Sharing your story offers a wealth of benefits. First, it allows others to see God's work through your eyes, providing new perspectives and encouragement. Have you ever shared a personal anecdote, only to hear someone say, "I needed to hear that today"? Your story has the power to inspire others. Plus, sharing opens up channels for deeper relationships. Suddenly, your tale of waiting becomes a communal experience, fostering bonds over shared faith journeys.

Building these connections doesn't necessarily mean standing on a soapbox and shouting your story to anyone who will listen. It can be as simple as sharing with a small group, writing a blog post, or even chatting with a friend over coffee. The beauty of sharing lies in its ability to make others feel seen and understood. You never know who might need a reminder that they're not alone in their waiting.

Now, let's talk tangible reminders. Creating a memory box is a fun and meaningful way to capture the physical evidence of God's faithfulness. Think of it as a treasure chest for your soul. Fill it with mementos of answered prayers, fulfilled hopes, and little tokens that remind you of significant moments. A ticket stub from an event you prayed about, a photo of a cherished moment, or even a note you wrote to yourself during a tough time—all these items become powerful symbols of God's promises kept.

This memory box isn't just for decoration; it serves as a touchstone for when doubts creep in. On days when faith feels like a distant echo, opening the box can reignite your spirit, reminding you of God's past kindnesses. It's like having a highlight reel of divine intervention right at your fingertips. And, of course, sharing these keepsakes with loved ones can foster deeper conversations and connections.

So, why does all this matter? Because understanding the journey of waiting enables us to see the broader picture of God's faithfulness. It's easy to get bogged down in daily struggles, but reflection, journaling, sharing, and creating physical reminders help anchor us in the truth of God's unwavering love. These practices turn abstract concepts of faith into concrete evidence, solidifying our trust in God and His timing.

In essence, embracing these methods can transform the way we perceive our spiritual journey. Instead of viewing waiting as a tedious intermission, we start to see it as a crucial chapter where growth happens, faith deepens, and God's character shines through. It's the difference between trudging through a dense forest aimlessly and navigating with a map that highlights every landmark, showing us exactly how far we've come and how much we've grown.

And let's be honest, we all need a bit of humor on this path. Life is too short to take our struggles too seriously. After all, laughter is a form of reflection too—a joyful acknowledgment that, despite everything, we're still here, still growing, and still supported by an ever-faithful God.

Giving Thanks and Testimonies

Gratitude is a powerful response to witnessing God's faithfulness, encouraging us to celebrate every fulfillment of His promises. By acknowledging God's blessings through gratitude, we shift our focus from what we lack to what has been provided for us. This simple act cultivates joy and resilience in our hearts. Think about it: when you're grateful, you naturally find more reasons to be joyful, even in circumstances that might otherwise bring you down. Imagine waking up each morning and choosing to see the blessings—the roof over your head, the food on your table, the air in your lungs. Suddenly, the day's challenges seem a bit smaller and more manageable.

Crafting a personal testimony about one's journey of waiting on God can also solidify the experience and serve as a powerful tool for evangelism and encouragement. Testimonies are like spiritual markers that remind us and others of God's faithfulness. They're stories that not only reinforce our own faith but inspire those who hear them. Sharing how you've seen God's hand at work, especially during tough times, can be incredibly uplifting. It's as if you're saying, "Look, if God brought me through this, He can do the same for you."

Integrating gratitude into daily routines can further instill a habit of celebration and enhance spiritual awareness and appreciation. Creating small rituals like writing in a gratitude journal or expressing thanks during prayer time can make a big difference. You could start by jotting down three things you're thankful for each day. Over time, these tiny moments of reflection add up, helping you to build a reservoir of positive memories and reinforcing your sense of divine provision. Taking a moment at dinner to share something good that happened during the day can turn an ordinary meal into an extraordinary act of worship.

Recognizing and celebrating significant milestones—be it publicly or privately—can encourage a spirit of joy and thanksgiving, creating traditions that endure. Whether it's a family gathering to celebrate a year of sobriety or a quiet evening reflecting on personal growth, marking these moments helps solidify their importance. Traditions give us something to look forward to and offer a deeper connection to God and each other. They're like mile markers along the journey of faith, pointing back to God's goodness and urging us onward with hope.

Let's consider some examples to make these points come alive. Picture Job in the Bible, who despite his immense suffering, chose to find gratitude. In Job 1:20-21, he says, "The Lord gave and the Lord has taken away; blessed be the name of the Lord." Job's story reminds us that gratitude doesn't ignore hardships but finds strength in the belief that blessings still exist amid the struggle (Lund, 2023). Similarly, King David often expressed his gratitude through psalms, focusing on who God is and what He has done.

We might sometimes overlook the small blessings in our lives because we're too focused on the next big thing. However, actively taking notice of what God is doing around us can be transformational. Consider starting a gratitude jar—each time something good happens, write it down on a slip of paper and drop it in. On harder days, reading these notes can provide a much-needed boost. It's incredible how such small acts can alter our outlook and remind us of God's continuous work in our lives (chrislawrence, 2021).

Creating a tradition of crafting personal testimonies is another way to embed gratitude into our lives. When you reflect on the hurdles you've overcome and recognize God's hand in them, you not only strengthen your own faith but also provide inspiration to others. Whether you're sharing these stories over coffee with a friend or speaking in front of a congregation, they serve as powerful reminders of God's faithfulness. Writing these down can also be beneficial. Imagine having a collection of journal entries that document your journey, which you can revisit whenever you need a reminder of God's goodness.

Developing a consistent practice of thanksgiving in prayers can also anchor us in a posture of gratitude. Psalm 100:4-5 encourages us to "enter His gates with thanksgiving and His courts with praise." By beginning our prayers with words of thanks, we set a tone of appreciation and acknowledgment of God's sovereignty. This habit can shift our focus from our problems to His provisions, enlarging our faith and trust in Him.

Celebrating milestones plays a critical role in fostering a spirit of thanksgiving and joy. For example, anniversaries, birthdays, or any major life accomplishment can be occasions for deliberate thankfulness. Hosting a small gathering or even taking a moment alone to thank God for the milestone can become valuable traditions. These celebrations don't have to be grand; even a simple gesture can hold profound meaning.

Incorporating these practices into our lives doesn't just change our perspective—it transforms our spiritual journey. By choosing gratitude, crafting our testimonies, integrating thanksgiving into everyday routines, and celebrating significant moments, we create a lifestyle rooted in joy and resilience. We begin to see God's hand more clearly in all aspects of our lives, reinforcing our trust in Him.

Using Fulfilled Promises to Inspire Future Faith

Reflecting on past fulfilled promises can be incredibly enriching, not just for reminiscing about good times but also for fortifying our faith in what lies ahead. Think of it like having a spiritual photo album. Each snapshot captures a moment when God came through for you or someone you know, and flipping through these pages regularly can significantly boost your trust and confidence in His future plans. It's almost like saying, "Look, if He did it before, He can do it again!" It turns waiting from a painful ordeal into an exciting preparation phase.

Biblical stories are chock-full of examples that highlight God's consistent and trustworthy nature. Take the story of Abraham and Sarah; they waited so long for a child that it seemed impossible. But God kept His promise, and Isaac was born. How about Moses leading the Israelites out of Egypt? Despite numerous obstacles, God's promises prevailed. These stories aren't just ancient text; they're living proof that God keeps His word. They serve as timeless encouragements, reminding us that His promises are rock-solid.

To make these fulfilled promises even more impactful, mentoring can be a fantastic approach. Sharing personal experiences of God's faithfulness with others who are currently waiting can be immensely powerful. Imagine you're a part of a small group at church, sharing the story of how you were once in a similar situation and how God fulfilled His promise to you. This doesn't just build individual faith; it fosters a sense of community. People start feeling less isolated in their struggles and more supported. It's a win-win for everyone involved, fostering mutual growth and encouragement.

Mentoring others is especially rewarding because it allows you to turn your experiences into valuable lessons for someone else. Maybe you waited for years for a job that aligns perfectly with your calling, and now you're mentoring a young graduate who's struggling to find their way. Your story becomes a beacon of hope, and your mentorship helps them navigate their own journey more confidently.

Setting faith-based future goals is another excellent strategy to keep the momentum going. Instead of just passively waiting for God's promises to unfold, why not take proactive steps? This could be as simple as incorporating specific prayers into your daily routine or setting small, achievable milestones that align with your faith journey. For instance, if you're hoping for a promotion at work, you could set a goal to improve certain skills that would make you a better candidate. It's about staying engaged and showing God that you're actively trusting Him. Goals like these not only keep your hopes alive but also help you maintain a positive and forward-thinking mindset.

Prayer is a crucial component of setting these goals. Regularly talking to God about your aspirations reinforces your commitment to His plans. When you make prayer an active part of your goal-setting process, you're essentially saying, "God, I trust You with this dream. Please guide me." This kind of active trust turns waiting into a dynamic engagement rather than a passive standstill.

Incorporating room for humor and light-hearted moments can also be incredibly beneficial. Life can be overwhelmingly serious, especially when we're in a season of waiting. A little laughter can go a long way in uplifting spirits. Remember the old saying, "Laughter is the best medicine"? It holds true in spiritual journeys too. Sharing funny anecdotes about your own experiences or finding joy in everyday moments can bring a refreshing perspective to a seemingly endless wait.

Imagine sharing a funny story during a mentoring session about how you tried to "help" God speed up His promises. Perhaps you went for a job interview you knew deep down wasn't right for you, thinking you could nudge the process along. In hindsight, it's hilarious, but at the time, it probably felt quite stressful. Sharing such stories brings a human element to the divine process, making it more relatable and less daunting.

The impact of humor isn't just limited to casual conversations. It can be incorporated into prayer and reflection too. Sometimes, acknowledging the absurdity of our own impatience can be liberating. It breaks the ice between us and God, making our relationship with Him even more genuine and open.

Summary and Reflections

As we wrap up our exploration of recognizing and celebrating the fulfillment of God's promises, let's take a moment to appreciate the journey we've been on together. We've looked at how reflecting on past experiences, whether through journaling, sharing stories, or creating memory boxes, helps us see God's faithfulness more clearly. By doing so, we turn abstract concepts into concrete reminders of His unwavering presence, making our faith journey feel more tangible and encouraging.

It's amazing how gratitude and testimonies can transform our perspectives. When we make a habit of giving thanks and sharing our stories, we not only uplift ourselves but also inspire those around us. Celebrating milestones and integrating gratitude into daily routines creates a lifestyle rooted in joy and resilience. Remember, life doesn't have to be all serious; a sprinkle of humor and acknowledging the lighter side of waiting can make this spiritual adventure even more enriching. So, let's hold tight to these practices, knowing that each fulfilled promise is a stepping stone toward greater faith and deeper connections with God and each other.

Conclusion

A s we come to the end of our journey together, it's essential to take a moment and reflect on what we've covered. We've delved into the depths of patience, exploring how waiting isn't just about twiddling our thumbs but an active part of our spiritual growth. Waiting on God, as we discovered, is like learning to dance in the rain rather than waiting for the storm to pass. It's about finding joy and purpose even when life has pressed pause.

In our first few chapters, we learned that patience is more than a virtue; it's a skill we cultivate. We likened it to gardening, where every seed planted in faith slowly sprouts with time and care. Our modern lives are so fast-paced that we often forget the beauty of watching things grow gradually. Each chapter was designed to remind us that slowing down and trusting the process can lead to profound spiritual insights.

Moving forward, think about the exercises and questions you tackled at the end of each chapter. These weren't mere assignments but stepping stones leading to personal revelations. Maybe you found out that your impatience stems from deeper anxieties or that your hurried lifestyle leaves little room for spiritual reflection. Whatever your discoveries, they form the backbone of your unique journey in mastering the art of waiting.

For instance, reflect on whether you've noticed a difference in your stress levels since practicing more intentional waiting. Have the breathing exercises helped during moments of frustration? Did writing in your journal unveil patterns about where impatience crops up most in your life? By revisiting these reflections, you gain a clearer understanding of where you began and how far you've come.

We also touched on the importance of community, an often overlooked yet vital part of navigating periods of waiting. A shared burden is a lightened load, and discussing your experiences with others can offer new perspectives and much-needed support. Whether it's a prayer group, a book club, or casual conversations over coffee, connecting with others who are also in seasons of waiting can be incredibly healing.

Now, think about your own circles. Who could benefit from your newfound insights? Maybe a friend who's struggling with relationship issues or a family member dealing with health concerns. Reaching out doesn't mean solving their problems but offering a listening ear and perhaps sharing your strategies for coping with periods of waiting. Sometimes, knowing someone else understands can make all the difference.

Let's not forget the actionable steps you can take moving forward. Integrating the principles discussed isn't about flipping a switch; it's about making gradual changes that align with your everyday life. Challenge yourself to view waiting as an opportunity rather than a setback. What proactive step can you take today to make your waiting period more meaningful?

Maybe you could start by setting small daily goals that connect to the bigger picture. If you're waiting for a career breakthrough, focus on enhancing your skills or expanding your network. If you're waiting for healing, explore ways to improve your well-being, both mentally and physically. Small steps create momentum, and before you know it, you'll find yourself making significant strides.

Think back to Chapter Nine, where we discussed embracing the "now" instead of always looking ahead. Embracing the present moment can transform your outlook. Try starting each day with a short meditation, grounding yourself in gratitude and focus. This simple practice can shift your mindset from one of impatience to one of contentment, making the wait feel less burdensome.

And don't overlook the power of prayer and spirituality in this process. Inviting God into your waiting period can transform it from a passive state to an active dialogue. Use this time to deepen your faith, whether through prayer, scripture reading, or reflective journaling. Ask yourself regularly, "What is God teaching me during this period of waiting?" Often, the lessons reveal themselves when we're open to receiving them.

If there's one thing I hope you take away from this book, it's that waiting doesn't have to be a dreaded interlude in the play of life. Instead, it can be a rich, transformative experience, full of hidden gems that contribute to your growth and understanding. Viewing waiting as an active, enriching process can fundamentally change your approach to life's inevitable pauses.

So, as you step back into your daily routines, challenge yourself to embrace waiting with a renewed perspective. Take proactive steps, engage in self-reflection, foster community connections, and most importantly, invite spiritual growth into your journey. Remember, waiting is not just a detour; it's a crucial part of the path.

Thank you for embarking on this journey with me. May your periods of waiting be filled with growth, discovery, and a touch of humor to lighten the load. Happy waiting!